"*Footsteps of Hope* is aptly titled. This book is more than a mother's sharing of the extremely painful loss of her only daughter; this book is a testimony of the ever-present healing grace of Almighty God for every circumstance of life lived in an imperfect world. He really is our fortress and high tower and when we run to Him as Sara did, God comes to us, wave after wave, with grace upon grace for our every need."

– Judie Foster

FOOTSTEPS OF HOPE

SARA FAITH NELSON

Printed in the United States of America
Published by Author Academy Elite
P.O. Box 43, Powell, OH 43035
www.AuthorAcademyElite.com

Unless otherwise indicated, all Scripture quotations are taken from the Holy Bible, New International Version®, NIV®. Copyright © 1973, 1978, 1984, 2011 by Biblica, Inc.™ Used by permission of Zondervan. All rights reserved worldwide. www.zondervan.com The "NIV" and "New International Version" are trademarks registered in the United States Patent and Trademark Office by Biblica, Inc.™

Scripture quotations marked (AMP) are taken from the Amplified Bible, Copyright © 1954, 1958, 1962, 1964, 1965, 1987 by The Lockman Foundation. Used by permission. www.Lockman.org.

Scripture quotations marked (MSG) are taken from THE MESSAGE, copyright © 1993, 1994, 1995, 1996, 2000, 2001, 2002 by Eugene H. Peterson. Used by permission of NavPress. All rights reserved. Represented by Tyndale House Publishers, Inc.

Scripture quotations marked (NKJV) are taken from the New King James Version®. Copyright © 1982 by Thomas Nelson. Used by permission. All rights reserved.

Scripture quotations marked (NLT) are taken from the Holy Bible, New Living Translation, copyright ©1996, 2004, 2007, 2013, 2015 by Tyndale House Foundation. Used by permission of Tyndale House Publishers, Inc., Carol Stream, Illinois 60188. All rights reserved.

What People Are Saying about *Footsteps of Hope*

"The words written in this book have touched my heart so deeply. As the mother of a child that has moved onto heaven, the loss is so deep that you no longer see a future. All you see is the loss that will always be there for the rest of your life. But Sara has pressed in and held onto the hope and future our Heavenly Father offers. As it has for me, this book will help you see hope for yourself once again. Thank you, Sara, for encouragement during our most difficult time."

– Dawn Tuthill

"As a bereaved parent, I so identify with Sara's experiences and so appreciate how she is allowing God to bring good from what seemed to be only bad after the loss of her precious daughter. Her devotional sharing is very encouraging and yet so real and vulnerable."

– Laurita Vodak

"I have not experienced losing a child but reading *Footsteps of Hope* helped me realize that I am still struggling with some of the effects of the loss of a young friend and the loss of a close grandmother. Not only did Sara help me see where I was still struggling with loss in my own life, her writing made me feel as if a friend had come to sit down next to me and help me work through it. She encouraged me by being honest about the uncomfortable subjects and struggles that she dealt with and by sharing the proactive steps she has taken to help on her own journey. I now realize that I am on my own specific path to healing and that I can take various combinations of actions unique to my journey to help along the way."

– Amber Dawn Stilwell

"Sara Nelson has beautifully captured the feelings of a bereaved parent. Any parent who has lost a child will be blessed by this devotional."

– Mary Diaz

"Sara Faith Nelson shares her personal journey of grief in a way that is encouraging for others who are grieving the death of a loved one. Sara shares her experience of the process of grief and her faith in God, as well as practical suggestions to help one survive and thrive through the heartbreak of grief and loss. Perhaps the most powerful message for other survivors is that "You are not alone." As a professional counselor, I would recommend this book as a source of understanding, encouragement, and hope for those who are grieving."

– Catherine Saffels

"Using the beautiful metaphor of a journey, with its accompanying mileposts, Sara Nelson has peeled back the layers of her heart to reveal not only the pain she has experienced in the loss of her daughter, but also the hope she has found from God's Word. I have no doubt that God will use this book, which often reads like the Psalms, to come alongside other grievers and reassure them that life does go on after the loss of a child—miraculously and beautifully—by God's amazing grace. This book will bring great hope and comfort to this broken world."

– Brenda Shipman

Scripture quotations marked (TPT) are from The Passion Translation®. Copyright © 2017, 2018 by Passion & Fire Ministries, Inc. Used by permission. All rights reserved. ThePassionTranslation.com.

Cover Design: Debbie O'Byrne
Photo Credit: Family photo by *Pauline Fredricks Photography*

This author has made a decision to capitalize pronouns for God (He, Him, His, etc.) as well as to capitalize Heaven as a proper noun, which may differ from the stylistic choice of others.

Library of Congress Control Number: 2019920017
ISBN: 978-1-64746-068-6 paperback
ISBN: 978-1-64746-069-3 hardcover
ISBN: 978-1-64746-070-9 ebook

Dedication
This book is dedicated to our beloved and precious daughter, Jeanette.

Our family: Sara, Dennis, and Jeanette

CONTENTS

PREFACE ... XXI

FOREWORD ... XXIII

INTRODUCTION ... XXVII

UNCHARTED TERRITORY

MILEPOST 1: ROADS AND ROLLER COASTERS ... 3

MILEPOST 2: THE EBB AND FLOW OF GRIEF ... 5

MILEPOST 3: LIFE GOES ON ... 7

MILEPOST 4: PERSPECTIVE ... 9

MILEPOST 5: EVERY TEAR A SEED ... 11

FOOTSTEPS IN UNCHARTED TERRITORY ... 12

TRAILBLAZING INTO THE WILDERNESS

MILEPOST 6: I CHOOSE LIFE	15
MILEPOST 7: GOOD DAYS AND BAD DAYS	17
MILEPOST 8: MY REFUGE AND STRENGTH	19
MILEPOST 9: NOT ALONE IN MY TROUBLES	21
MILEPOST 10: LIFE GOES ON: A REMINDER	23
FOOTSTEPS FOR TRAILBLAZING INTO THE WILDERNESS	25

TANGLED JUNGLES

MILEPOST 11: ANGER	29
MILEPOST 12: POISONOUS PITY	33
MILEPOST 13: FROM WRESTLING TO RESOLUTION	35
MILEPOST 14: PHYSICAL SIDE EFFECTS OF GRIEF	39
MILEPOST 15: SOMETIMES I NEED TO STOP FIGHTING SO HARD	43
FOOTSTEPS THROUGH THE TANGLED JUNGLES	45

HILLS AND VALLEYS

MILEPOST 16 : HEALING FOR AN INTROVERT'S SOUL	49

MILEPOST 17: HOPE, IDENTITY, AND SIGNIFICANCE	51
MILEPOST 18: HOPE, PURPOSE, AND A FUTURE	53
MILEPOST 19: WHAT IS A NEW NORMAL?	55
MILEPOST 20: MY GRIEF JOURNEY, FOUR MONTHS IN	57
FOOTSTEPS OVER THE HILLS AND VALLEYS	60

RUGGED TRAILS

MILEPOST 21: GOD'S PRESENCE QUIETS MY FEARS	65
MILEPOST 22: SOMETIMES BAD NEWS COMES	67
MILEPOST 23: WHAT TO DO ABOUT MOTHER'S DAY AND FATHER'S DAY	71
MILEPOST 24: GOD SURROUNDS ME WITH HIS LOVE	73
MILEPOST 25: PRESSING ON	75
FOOTSTEPS OVER ROUGH TERRAIN	77

SCENIC OVERLOOKS

MILEPOST 26: PERMISSION TO ENJOY THINGS AGAIN	81
MILEPOST 27: REFLECTIONS ON OLD AND NEW	83
MILEPOST 28: THE MENTION OF HER NAME	85

MILEPOST 29: AT THE SIX-MONTH MILEPOST	87
MILEPOST 30: BUILDING BRIDGES ON THE JOURNEY	89
FOOTSTEPS THAT MEASURE PROGRESS	91

ARE WE THERE YET?

MILEPOST 31: MILES TO GO BEFORE I SLEEP	95
MILEPOST 32: HEAVEN IS FOR REAL	97
MILEPOST 33: MY CONCEPT OF HEAVEN AND HOW IT'S CHANGED	99
MILEPOST 34: LIVING IN A WORLD WITHOUT HER	103
MILEPOST 35: HOPE OF HEAVEN	105
FOOTSTEPS TOWARD HEAVEN	107

STEEP TERRAIN

MILEPOST 36: OUR FIRST THANKSGIVING IN A NEW WORLD	111
MILEPOST 37: ONE CHRISTMAS AT A TIME	115
MILEPOST 38: MILEPOSTS AND TOLL ROADS	117
MILEPOST 39: THAT DAY	119

MILEPOST 40: FINDING NORMAL IS LIKE SEARCHING FOR NEVER-NEVER LAND	121
FOOTSTEPS FOR THE HARDEST DAYS OF THE YEAR	123

TAR PITS AND OTHER HAZARDS

MILEPOST 41: STUCK IN THE TAR PIT OF GRIEF	129
MILEPOST 42: VOLCANOES	131
MILEPOST 43: STAYING BALANCED ON THE TEETER-TOTTER OF GRIEF	133
MILEPOST 44: THE SERENITY PRAYER	135
MILEPOST 45: CONVALESCING	137
FOOTSTEPS FOR ESCAPING THE MIRE	139

TWISTS AND TURNS

MILEPOST 46: ANESTHETICS	143
MILEPOST 47: LETTING GO	145
MILEPOST 48: THE HALF-FULL GLASS	147
MILEPOST 49: MY GRIEF JOURNEY AT EIGHTEEN MONTHS	149
MILEPOST 50: TRANSITION	151

| FOOTSTEPS FOR WAYWARD JOURNEYS | 153 |

ENDURANCE TESTS

MILEPOST 51: PICKING UP THE PIECES ONE BY ONE	157
MILEPOST 52: WHAT NO ONE EVER TOLD ME ABOUT GRIEF	159
MILEPOST 53: SOARING ON EAGLE'S WINGS	161
MILEPOST 54: TRUTH THAT GIVES HOPE	163
MILEPOST 55: TAPESTRY	165
FOOTSTEPS FOR THE LONG HAUL	167

STEPPING STONES

MILEPOST 56: BEING THANKFUL EVEN IN GRIEF	171
MILEPOST 57: ACCEPTING THE BITTERSWEET	173
MILEPOST 58: HOPE SPRINGS ETERNAL	175
MILEPOST 59: MAKING THE MOST OF THE DASH	177
MILEPOST 60: REFLECTIONS ON THE SECOND ANNIVERSARY OF JEANETTE'S HEAVEN-GOING	179
FOOTSTEPS FROM ONE YEAR TO THE NEXT	181

SHAKY GROUND

MILEPOST 61: SHUTTING THE DOOR ON FEAR	185
MILEPOST 62: PESKY EMOTIONS	187
MILEPOST 63: I PRESS ON	189
MILEPOST 64: WHEN JOY BECOMES OUR STRENGTH	191
MILEPOST 65: SURFING MOTHER'S DAY	193
FOOTSTEPS TO STEADY OUR FEET	195

CHECKING THE MAP

MILESTONE 66: BROKEN BUT STILL SMILING	199
MILESTONE 67: RECALCULATING	201
MILEPOST 68: WHAT'S NEXT, PAPA?	203
MILEPOST 69: HEAVENLY PERSPECTIVE	205
MILEPOST 70: WWJD?	207
FOOTSTEPS FOR ADVENTURERS	209

SHADOWY PATHWAYS

MILEPOST 71: CANYONS	213

MILEPOST 72: WHAT TO DO WITH CHRISTMAS WHEN THE WHOLE WORLD IS AWRY	215
MILEPOST 73: TUNNELS	217
MILESTONE 74: ANOTHER BIRTHDAY IN HEAVEN	219
MILEPOST 75: ANOTHER ANNIVERSARY OF THAT DAY	221
FOOTSTEPS TOWARD THE LIGHT	223

ROCKY ROADS

MILEPOST 76: LIFE IS A BOUNCY HOUSE	227
MILEPOST 77: UNSHAKABLE	229
MILEPOST 78: BEREAVED MOTHER'S DAY	231
MILEPOST 79: WHAT I WANT FOR MOTHER'S DAY	233
MILEPOST 80: NO ONE TO CALL ME GRANDMA	235
FOOTSTEPS FOR OVERCOMING	237

POUNDING THE PAVEMENT

MILEPOST 81: WASH, RINSE, REPEAT	241
MILEPOST 82: THE WILL TO LIVE	243
MILESTONE 83: FESTIVUS — THE GRIEVER'S EDITION	245

MILEPOST 84: LET THE WEAK SAY, "I AM STRONG"	249
MILEPOST 85: SECRETS TO SURVIVAL	251
FOOTSTEPS FOR WEARY TRAVELERS	254

CROSSROADS

MILEPOST 86: ASKING WHY	257
MILEPOST 87: HOW CAN I POSSIBLY BELIEVE GOD IS GOOD?	261
MILEPOST 88: EARTH'S GRIEF AND HEAVEN'S GLORY	265
MILEPOST 89: GRIEF SUPPORT GROUPS	267
MILEPOST 90: LIFE'S DEFINING MOMENTS	271
FOOTSTEPS TO SURVIVE AND THRIVE	274
ACKNOWLEDGMENTS	277
ABOUT THE AUTHOR	279
COMING BOOKS BY SARA FAITH NELSON	280
RECOMMENDED RESOURCES	281
REFERENCES	283

PREFACE

Every grief journey is as unique as a fingerprint. No two people experience it the same way, yet our footsteps cover enough common ground to enable us to find comfort, encouragement, and hope in sharing our journey and our stories. My story begins in 2014 after my daughter's Heaven-going when I began journaling, blogging, and posting on social media about my grief journey. This book was birthed from those writings.

One of the things I've discovered in common with other grievers is how our grief journey is not a straight line from point to point, but rather, we tend to circle back around and seemingly cover the same ground over and over. You'll see this throughout my journey. However, there's always an upward trend. We're not going around and around in circles on the same path. Every time we go around the mountain, we're a little bit higher. Repetition uncovers new insights as we advance upward and every round brings fresh healing.

Since mileposts measure our progress as we travel, this book is separated into Mileposts with five Mileposts in each section. Each section closes with a Footstep to aid you in your personal journey. I recommend journaling along with this book. We walk this journey at our own pace, finding the path that's best for us, and journaling will help you find your own way through your grief. Record your own mileposts and the discoveries that renew, refresh, and revive your hope and strength. It will not only be helpful for you, but one day, you may find yourself comforting others with the comfort you have received.

"Praise be to the God and Father of our Lord Jesus Christ, the Father of compassion and the God of all comfort, who comforts us in all our troubles, so that we can comfort those in any trouble with the comfort we ourselves receive from God. For just as we share abundantly in the sufferings of Christ, so also our comfort abounds through Christ" (2 Corinthians 1:3–5).

FOREWORD

When you find out someone is a fellow believer in Christ, doesn't it seem like you just found instant "family?" It is the same way with us as bereaved parents. We are instantly bonded as "family," no matter how different our beliefs in religion, politics, or any other area. And sometimes we are blessed with more than just discovering a new family member, we discover a new life-long friend. That is how I feel about Sara Nelson.

Sara and I "met" online, through one of our GPS Hope resources. It quickly developed into a friendship, so much so that along with our husbands, we chanced meeting half-way between Wisconsin and Arizona to share a condo for a five-day vacation in Branson, MO as the first time we met face-to-face. Fortunately, this time together solidified our God-ordained relationship!

My husband, Dave, and I started GPS Hope (Grieving Parents Sharing Hope) three years after the death of our oldest daughter. Becca needed a heart transplant that had been damaged by chemotherapy when only three years old. (Her treatment also included having her little left leg amputated.) The heart damage plagued her for the last ten years of her life, and the last eighteen months included three med flight helicopter rides and a dozen ambulance rides.

Ironically, the same drug that saved her life as a child is what ended her life, twenty-six years later, on October 12, 2011. Besides Dave and I, Becca also left behind a husband, a nine-year-old daughter, four siblings, a sister-in-law and a niece, along with all four of her grandparents.

As you will read in the following pages, Sara lost her adult daughter, Jeanette, from this earth as well. But there is a big difference, in that Jeanette was Sara and Dennis' *only* child and Jeanette had no children. (I cannot imagine what that would be like, and my heart aches for those in a similar situation.)

As bereaved parents, all our stories are different, our grief looks different and where we will end up is different. But we are all on the same path of deep loss, and the only way to get through the darkness and out to the other side is to keep putting one step in front of the other, no matter how small those steps may be.

Losing a child is like having an amputation (and we know a lot about that from Becca). Part of your very being has been cut off from you, and you must figure out how to live with that piece of you missing. At the beginning, we don't think that is even possible, but Sara and I are here to tell you that it is. You *can* learn how to live a life of meaning and purpose again, not in spite of your child's death, but because of his or her life.

In *Footsteps of Hope*, you will discover how Sara has been able to do this, in a way that will guide you in your own journey. Knowing Sara, her journey and her writing abilities, I wasn't surprised to discover some golden nuggets myself, while reading it.

I am not going to sugar coat it; the journey is long and hard, but it is so much better when we are not walking it alone. Sara Nelson has followed in my footsteps of hope, and in the same way, I pray that you will follow hers, and then go on in your own way to make footsteps of hope for someone else.

Laura Diehl

Award-winning author of *When Tragedy Strikes*, speaker/singer, cofounder of Grieving Parents Sharing Hope (www.gpshope.org)

INTRODUCTION

No parent should ever have to write their child's obituary. But that's the task that fell to me. As I drafted the obituary for our daughter, it felt like the most important words I would ever write. I'd like to share part of it to introduce Jeanette to you. She was our only child, my best friend, and the light of my life.

Jeanette Marie, 1978–2014

Jeanette joined family and friends in Heaven, Sunday, February 9. Her departure from us was too sudden and too soon, but we are greatly consoled by picturing her arrival through the gates of Heaven and the welcome she received.

Jeanette leaves a legacy of love and kindness, generosity and helpfulness, creativity and talent, humor and laughter. As a teacher, she deeply touched the lives of her students. She is remembered as a teacher who truly loved and cared for each child. The imprint of her life lives on in them. Jeanette would be amazed to know how far her sphere of influence reaches and how many lives will never be the same for knowing her.

Growing up as an "army brat," she made many lasting friendships. She enjoyed many places we lived but loved Germany most of all. Visiting museums, castles, and historic sites built a strong love of history and art, which influenced her decision to major in history and minor in art history in college.

Jeanette was beginning to explore her artistic talents in sketching and art journaling. She was creative in crafts of all kinds, plus photography and crochet. She loved nature. Our family camping trips were a staple of her childhood. She also loved to cook and had a wonderful gift of hospitality. For a life so shortly lived, Jeanette blessed many, many people. She is—and will be—greatly missed by all who knew her.

After writing Jeanette's obituary, I wrote additional thoughts to be shared at her memorial service. It provides some background about what happened and our thoughts about Jeanette's passing in the immediate days following her Heaven-going.

We are celebrating Jeanette's 36 years of life today as we gather to remember her. We've been grieving her loss, and we will continue to mourn, but for right now, today, we celebrate the fact that she lived. We cherish the blessing of who she was and our precious memories of her.

God knew the number of her days before any yet came to be. Although we were taken by surprise the day she left her earthly life behind, it was not a surprise to God. In many ways, God prepared us in advance even though we didn't realize what was to come. Probably the biggest preparation began last February when Jeanette had her first seizure. I've never seen anyone have a seizure before, and I didn't know what was happening. I was terrified! I called 9-1-1, screaming into my phone in panic. Sitting in the front seat of the ambulance on the way to the hospital, all I could think was, "God, I can't go on without her." He heard my prayer and granted us one more year.

Results of tests for the cause of her seizures came back "inconclusive." We never found out for sure what caused them. After another seizure, she and her husband (Joe) moved in with us because it made things easier. She would get exasperated with me always asking if she was okay. I couldn't help it. My mom-radar was on high alert. Months passed, and there were no more seizures. We were just beginning to relax, thinking we could close the book on that chapter, but then, another seizure happened, and our hopes crashed. That's when I knew in my gut something was terribly wrong.

On Sunday, February 9, I received a frantic phone call from a friend, telling us that Jeanette had collapsed, and they had called an ambulance. We rushed over just in time to see her body on a gurney as paramedics took her from the house. Numb with shock and disbelief, we followed the ambulance to the hospital. Dazed. Confused. Hoping against hope. The hospital ER team worked on her, but even without being told, we knew she was already gone. Friends came and sat by our side, praying for us. My prayers felt like lead. and the only thought in my mind was, "How could this be happening?"

It was almost a year to the day since her first seizure. A year ago, I cried out to God that I couldn't live without her, and He mercifully granted us one more year. One more year to be blessed with her presence. One more year to cherish. One more year to prepare for what we didn't know was coming.

The first question everyone asks is why. Why did this happen? Why, God, why? Of all the big questions, this one feels the heaviest, most ponderous, most burdensome, of all. And yet, in these few short days since her passing, the question of why pales in comparison to the love and goodness of God. We have an amazing peace that defies description and all reason. As we look toward the future, we know it will not be easy. The hole in our lives and in our hearts can never be filled. And yet, we also know that God's love is immeasurably more than we can ask or imagine, and His grace is more than enough, even for this.

Our message to all of you who loved Jeanette dearly and will miss her deeply is not to despair. Trust God to bring something beautiful out of our loss, because He is faithful, and He will keep His promise to give us "beauty for ashes, the oil of joy for mourning, the garment of praise for the spirit of heaviness" (Isaiah 61:3 NKJV).

A few days after Jeanette's memorial, I wrote this in my journal:

Our lives continue without Jeanette. The memorial service is past. All the guests have gone home. Dennis is back to work. It feels like today is the first official day of a new life's journey. Today we begin our quest for a new normal.

With my coffee at hand, I write in my journal and talk with God. I have such a sense of peace and hope for the days ahead. Amazing! Who would have thought it possible? I would not have imagined I could weather this loss. The peace within me is from God, through and through.

Jeanette's absence is deeply, keenly felt. Oh, how she is missed! Yet there is also such a soft and gentle sweetness, like her kiss upon our lives. It's indescribable! Life goes on, and I know it can still be good.

The most Jeanette-honoring thing we can do is to live our life and live it well. Be more alive than we've ever been before. Enjoy life more than we ever have before. Make the most of each and every day, more than we ever have before. Look ahead with eyes focused on the future, not the past. Cherish the memories but embrace life.

UNCHARTED TERRITORY
WHERE THE JOURNEY BEGINS, SCRAMBLING TO FIND OUR WAY IN A PLACE WE HAVE NEVER BEEN BEFORE

MILEPOST 1
ROADS AND ROLLER COASTERS

Life is full of ups and downs. We don't always have a choice how rough or smooth life will be. But we do have a choice of road or roller coaster. The difference is a road leads to a destination, but a roller coaster goes nowhere. – My journal entry, January 2014.

I wrote those words in my journal scarcely more than a month before being propelled on a journey I never intended, never wanted, and would never have chosen. More than ever, I ponder the choice set before me: road or roller coaster? If I must endure the wild ups and downs of grief, I'd rather be on a road that takes me somewhere instead of a roller coaster that goes nowhere.

The course of this journey certainly feels like a wild roller coaster ride, but I prefer to think of it as a winding, twisty road with many hills and valleys. I do not know the destination or the purpose for being on this road. Even though I don't see a purpose yet, I resolutely believe there is one. Therefore, I choose not to despair, not to sink into the abyss of sorrow and drown there. No! I press onward to discover where the road leads.

God brings assurance that no matter what happens in life, even the traumas and tragedies, He can turn it around for good. (See Genesis 50:20 and Romans 8:28.) The only way to find out how that will happen is to keep on going.

"'For I know the plans I have for you,' declares the LORD, 'plans to prosper you and not to harm you, plans to give you hope and a future'" (Jeremiah 29:11). When it's hard to trust God and hard to believe there's a plan, a purpose, a future, or a hope, I cling to this verse. God's plan for me is good even through the twists and turns on the road of life.

Imagining anything positive about the future is difficult in the early days, weeks, and months after loss, and yet it's so vital to rekindling hope. Make an effort today to speak hope into your future, trusting that God will bring healing to your wounded heart.

MILEPOST 2
THE EBB AND FLOW OF GRIEF

We have this hope as an anchor for the soul, firm and secure (Hebrews 6:19a).

The name of the LORD is a strong tower; the righteous run to it and are safe (Proverbs 18:10, NKJV).

Even though I'm still new to grief, I'm already figuring out that it comes like ocean waves. I've only had an opportunity to live near an ocean once in my life. I loved going to the beach and wading into the surf. Sometimes the waves were scary, though. I could feel the pull of the surf and I could see the ocean rising as a wave approached. I was afraid I might not be strong enough—what if I were to drown?—as the wave lifted me and carried me along with it. But then, when the wave passed, my feet would touch solid ground again.

Waves of grief can seem overwhelming, just like the ocean waves, and I fear drowning in my grief. But the wave passes, and I touch solid ground again. Another wave builds. I anticipate it and dread it. But it, too, passes. Wave by wave, I'm getting through it. Wave by wave, I'm keeping my head above water.

The ebb and flow of grief grants me a respite now and then. Some days it doesn't feel quite as bad. Then the tide turns, and emotions rise again. I suppose I will live with this ebb and flow of grief for the rest of my life. I dread these high-tide days when strong emotions threaten to overwhelm me.

I've read that sailors, in the days of the old sailing ships, would climb into the rigging and wrap themselves in the ropes to keep from being swept overboard by stormy waves flooding the ship's deck. That picture comes to mind when emotions surge over me. I climb to my place of safety, my strong tower, my refuge in the Lord.

Waves of grief come and go. They do not stay. One wave at a time, we survive. God will not let us drown. He is an anchor, a solid rock, and a strong tower when the waves of grief overwhelm us. Meditate on hope as an anchor, firm and secure, when those waves come.

MILEPOST 3
LIFE GOES ON

I remain confident of this: I will see the goodness of the LORD in the land of the living. Wait for the LORD, be strong and take heart and wait for the LORD (Psalm 27:13–14).

Life goes on, whether we feel like it or not. The sunrise of each new day brings a fresh wave of sadness, and yet life goes on. The hurt I feel is so deep, and yet life *still* goes on. I try to find something positive each day *because* life goes on.

I need courage to face each new day. I'm still reeling from the shock of what happened, still trying to wrap my mind around it. But every day, the sun rises anew. Every day is a fresh opportunity to heal, to grow, and to come to terms with her death a little bit more.

Everyone else might go on with their lives as always, but for me, my world has come to a standstill. How can the sun continue to rise and set as if all is normal? How dare life go on! But what a picture of hope that each dawn ushers in a fresh, new day. If the world can keep spinning, and the sun, moon, and stars stay in their orbits without crashing, maybe life can go on. Just as every night gives way to morning light, the darkness will eventually retreat.

In spite of the huge hole in my heart and in my life, I am surprised to discover there are still blessings. God is with me through every aching moment. Friends encourage and comfort me in a multitude of ways. The march of life continues, and I follow its path, trusting for better days ahead.

MILEPOST 4
PERSPECTIVE

I keep my eyes always on the LORD. With him at my right hand, I will not be shaken (Psalm 16:8).

It's up to me to choose my perspective:

- Every morning I wake up, and Jeanette's not here.

or

- Every morning I wake up, and God is with me.

Both statements are true, but only one leads to hope; the other, to despair. When I wake up each day, I choose one or the other—to focus on her absence or God's presence.

Perspective is everything. Whatever I focus on most affects my outlook. If I focus on the darkness of my grief, I am overwhelmed by it. I drown in it. It's too much to bear. But if I turn my attention to God, no matter how badly I feel, I see pinpoints of light in the darkness. I see small blessings of comfort throughout the day.

Right this minute, I am looking at a rainbow of light from a prism hanging on a wind chime outside my front door. The colorful reflection dances across the living room ceiling as the prism pirouettes in the morning breeze. But the rainbow of colors only lasts a short time while the angle of the sun catches it. If I'm not looking, I miss it.

I don't take even a small gift, such as a cheerful reflection of light, for granted. I need every bit of light and brightness I can gather into my heart to soothe its perpetual ache. I'm thankful for every small thing. I set my eyes on God, and I will not be shaken.

Emotions of grief can be so strong they drown out everything else. It's easy to lose touch with God's presence and wonder where He is or if He's with us at all. At such times, tangible objects, such as the prism on my wind chime, are helpful in reminding us of His love and promises to never leave us or forsake us. A simple object placed where we see it daily can help to remind us that even in the darkness of grief, God is with us.

MILEPOST 5
EVERY TEAR A SEED

Those who sow in tears will reap with songs of joy. Those who go out weeping, carrying seeds to sow, will return with songs of joy, carrying sheaves with them (Psalm 126:5–6).

For now, my vision is dimmed by the tears, but I pray my tears will fall on good soil and return a harvest of good fruit. I don't consider it merely wishful thinking to believe something good can grow from this place of pain. To look beyond what I can see right now requires faith—faith to see the harvest while still sowing the seed.

Trusting that something worthwhile can come from this pain is essential. To keep putting one foot in front of the other day after day, to go on living, to see the years of my life spreading out in front of me like a long and rugged road before I arrive at Heaven's gate, I must know there's a purpose. I cling to the promise of good fruit and a great harvest for such a dear price as my daughter's life.

Footsteps in Uncharted Territory

It's been said that to plant a seed is to believe in the future. Think about how true that is. Growing a memory garden is a project with so many variations practically anyone can find a version to suit them—indoors or outdoors, simple or elaborate. Gardening in any of its forms, even tending to a houseplant, is a worthwhile project. Dedicating it to our dear loved one can be a healing and therapeutic activity.

Gardening is not really my thing and Arizona can be a challenging place for gardeners. But, in the spring after Jeanette died, I wanted to plant something in an unused flower bed, a spot where I'd previously been unsuccessful getting anything to grow. When I began working on that flower bed, it inspired my husband to clear a space nearby and lay down paver stones for a patio. Five years later, we have a beautiful, peaceful sitting area. English Ivy is thriving in that flower bed. A variety of birds come to bird feeders. LED lights twinkle at night. Now and then we find something new to add to the space. It's been such a blessing to both my husband and me. Every person's memory garden will be different, depending on where you live and other variables. But I encourage you to consider the possibilities for your situation.

As you tend your garden, pray this:

Dear God, may every tear be a seed that will bring a harvest of good fruit. If I must endure this pain, make it useful. Don't let it be in vain. Turn my tears into a catalyst that propels me forward into something I might not have otherwise become or into a destiny I would not have otherwise found.

"He has made everything beautiful in its time" (Ecclesiastes 3:11a).

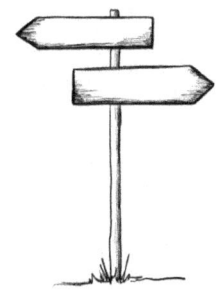

TRAILBLAZING INTO THE WILDERNESS

HOW TO COPE WITH GRIEF AS WE'VE NEVER KNOWN IT BEFORE

MILEPOST 6
I CHOOSE LIFE

I'm on a diet of tears—tears for breakfast, tears for supper. All day long [my thoughts] knock at my door, pestering, 'Where is this God of yours?' ...Sometimes I ask God, my rock-solid God, 'Why did you let me down? Why am I walking around in tears?' ...Why are you down in the dumps, dear soul? Why are you crying the blues? Fix my eyes on God— soon I'll be praising again. He puts a smile on my face. He's my God (Psalm 42:3, 9, 11 MSG). (Brackets indicate a word substitution.)

This morning, I saw a cloud that looked like a stick-figure person with outstretched arms like someone ready to give me a big hug. My first thought was, "Oh, look at that! Jeanette is hugging me from Heaven! How sweet!" But another thought immediately followed. "It's just a stupid cloud! It means nothing!"

My emotions immediately darkened. My heart sank into a dark place of cold numbness, not the least bit comforting. It felt as if a black cloud moved across my mind, turning my heart into a cold, wind-swept wasteland. "No!" I shouted out loud. "I will not go there!"

With deliberate intention, I turned my thoughts away from that dark place. I looked up at the sky again. The Jeanette-cloud had moved on, but the deep azure sky was filled with many more billowy clouds. I concentrated on the warm spring air, budding trees, and singing birds. The calming sweetness of God's presence soon permeated my mind, replacing the darkness.

Once more, I am aware of the importance of choice. It's my choice to accept simple, sweet gifts, like the Jeanette-cloud hugging me from the heavens. It's my choice to turn from the dark, cold numbness to an awareness of beauty and light. The loneliness of grief is still with me, but it's my choice whether I let it pull me down into a dark pit or focus on beauty, light, and life.

Grief tells me there's a hole in my heart. God tells me I am whole in Him. Grief points to what's missing in my life. God points to how full and overflowing I am in Him. Today I choose to believe beauty, light, and life will return. I choose life!

MILEPOST 7
GOOD DAYS AND BAD DAYS

He lifted me out of the ditch, pulled me from deep mud. He stood me up on a solid rock to make sure I wouldn't slip. He taught me how to sing the latest God-song, a praise-song to our God (Psalm 40:2–3 MSG).

There's no way to get to the other side of grief without slogging through the mud and the muck of difficult emotions, but even in the mire, God is with me. He holds me up and keeps me from slipping into the darkness of despair. He helps me navigate through the murky places so I don't get stuck there. He sets my feet on solid ground again.

I'm thankful for good days, but bad days are part of the territory. Grief is not something that can be bypassed, no matter how much I'd like to. I may have to slog through it, but I don't have to wallow in it. I thank God for helping me through the mire, picking me up when I slip and fall, and for multiplying my good days.

There's something to be said for faith that perseveres no matter what and believes in light when there is no light. There is power in persisting in faith despite the darkness. Faith such is this does not go unnoticed and carries great reward. Don't give up.

MILEPOST 8
MY REFUGE AND STRENGTH

In You, O LORD, I have put my trust and confidently taken refuge... Be to me a rock of refuge and a sheltering stronghold to which I may continually come... For You are my hope; O Lord GOD, You are my trust and the source of my confidence from my youth (Psalm 71:1, 3, 5 AMP).

I've been fighting feelings of depression, fighting with everything in me. Sadness is one thing, but depression is another. I can relieve some of the sadness with a satisfying cry, but depression is different. It feels like an overwhelming darkness trying to swallow and consume me. It's like being on the brink of a swirling vortex, like being pulled into a black hole against my will. I'm resisting it with all my might. I don't want it! I won't accept it! I refuse! Yet for all my resistance, I'm being dragged into it anyway.

They say depression is a normal part of grieving, but I don't like feeling this way. If this is my new normal,

I don't want it! There's a lot about this new normal I don't like. This is not how my life is supposed to be. I guess that's the root of what I'm resisting: the fact that my life has turned upside down and coping with grief has become normal. I'm angry that grief, sadness, and depression are in my life.

But as I read Psalm 71, I am reminded of all the hardships and difficult times I've faced in my life. Nothing in the past comes close to the devastating loss of Jeanette, but it's not as if I've never been in rough, uncharted waters before. And in all those times past, God stood with me to give me strength. There is not one time in my life when God wasn't there for me. God has strengthened me and helped me get through every struggle and hardship I've ever faced. This Psalm reminded me that God is still with me. He hasn't forsaken me. God is my refuge and my strength even now.

MILEPOST 9
NOT ALONE IN MY TROUBLES

Surely He has borne our griefs and carried our sorrows (Isaiah 53:4a NKJV).

For we do not have a high priest who is unable to empathize with our weaknesses (Hebrews 4:15a).

If we don't know how or what to pray, it doesn't matter. He does our praying in and for us, making prayer out of our wordless sighs, our aching groans (Romans 8:26b MSG).

Yesterday for a fleeting moment, I thought this grief thing was becoming easier. Today I'm down at the bottom of the depths. Tomorrow I'll likely be back up again. I need sea-sickness medicine for all these ups and downs.

The voyage through grief is indeed a rough and stormy sea. I'm so thankful we are not alone. I'm so thankful that God is not merely watching from a distance, impersonally looking on without any concern or compassion while we go through this. To the contrary, He is personally invested in us. God sent His Son, Jesus, to carry our grief. He knows grief firsthand because He Himself experienced sorrow. The Holy Spirit, our Comforter, is even now interceding for us with feelings so intense, there are no human words. Yes, grief is a stormy sea, but we are not alone. I'm thankful God feels our pain. He cares about us. And we have the whole Trinity holding onto us, so we won't drown in these troubled waters.

MILEPOST 10
LIFE GOES ON: A REMINDER

I'm the last person—the very last person—anyone would expect to get a tattoo. Not that I had any religious objection about tattoos, as some do, but I couldn't see much sense in the whole tattoo-craze, and I admit to being a little grossed out by the whole tattooing process. Then Jeanette died, and I began to think about tattoos in an entirely new way. Suddenly they did make sense. What a significant way to remember a much-loved person. I took a simple sketch of what I wanted to a tattoo artist and she created something beautiful: a red rose, hearts, Jeanette's name, and the words, life goes on.

Those three words—life goes on—are a reminder that only Jeanette's earthly life came to an end. In Heaven, she is more alive than I am. But those words are also my lifeline every day. I never would have chosen this path of grief. But I wasn't given a choice. Since I can't change it, I'd rather look forward than backward. I'd rather focus on the sunshine than the shadows. I'd rather see potential, and even dare to dream a new dream. I'd rather continue this journey to see what's around the next bend and where it leads. I will only know by taking one step at a time. One foot in front of the other. One day at a time. *Life goes on.*

Footsteps for Trailblazing into the Wilderness

Grief and loss can easily overshadow everything. It can drain every vestige of light and hope until all we see is darkness. That's why it is so essential to do whatever we can to fuel our faith, our trust, and our vision for a better future.

Romans 4:17 tells about Abraham believing in God's promise, even though he didn't see any sign of it coming to pass. People often quote a portion of this verse admonishing us to "speak of those things that be not as though they are." This doesn't mean denying reality. Rather, it's simply speaking with faith for what we don't see or don't yet have, as in Hebrews 11:1. The Message Bible says it this way. "When everything was hopeless, Abraham believed anyway, deciding to live not on the basis of what he saw he *couldn't* do but on what God said he *would* do" (Romans 4:17b, MSG) (Also see 2 Corinthians 4:13–18.) It is a walk of faith to believe there are better, brighter days ahead when all we see right now is the darkness of our grief.

Journaling is an excellent way to work through questions, doubts, and negativity. In addition, journaling is a great workspace for brainstorming strategies for difficult days. Below is a list of ideas to start with. These aren't a cure-all, by any means, but they can provide a respite for a short while. After you've made your list, choose something to do today.

- Go for a walk.
- Begin a hobby.
- Work on your memory garden.
- Complete one small project around the house.
- Listen to music.
- Sketch, draw, paint, or color a picture.

- Make a scrapbook page in your journal related to your grief journey.
- Meet a friend for coffee or lunch.
- Browse in your favorite store (mine is Hobby Lobby).
- Lose yourself in the pages of a book.
- Watch a funny movie.
- Soak in a bubble bath.

What can you think of to add to this list?

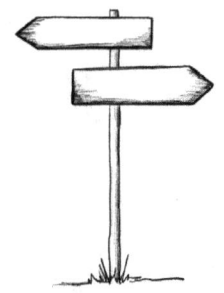

TANGLED JUNGLES
WHEN THE NUMBNESS WEARS OFF AND REALITY IS HARD TO BEAR

MILEPOST 11
ANGER

Go ahead and be angry. You do well to be angry—but don't use your anger as fuel for revenge. And don't stay angry. Don't go to bed angry. Don't give the Devil that kind of foothold in your life (Ephesians 4:26–27 MSG).

I let the dam burst. I rage! I yell! I sob on my knees and pound my fists into the carpet; I say all the things on my mind to say. I let loose the storm of pent-up blame, all the whys, all the regrets, all the guilt, all the frustration of what I couldn't control, and every factor that played some role in her death. Oh, how I wish I could roll back time and undo every one of those things! I wish I could make it turn out differently, yet I know that's not within my power.

Anger is my emotion de jour. I felt it rising in me like a tsunami. I couldn't keep it bottled up any longer. Anger may be part of the grieving process, but I don't like it. It's distasteful, unpleasant, and ugly. And yet, I need to let it out in order to let it go. I must release and send away this bitter feeling that keeps welling up inside me.

When all is said and done, the fury in me subsides and gives way to cleansing tears. With the tears, I allow forgiveness to enter. Forgiveness is the healing balm my soul needs, regardless of what anyone should have or could have done differently. Most of all, I forgive myself: for not knowing, not seeing, not being aware of what she needed, and for not being able to save her.

I know it's been said before, but it's the truth—unforgiveness makes us bitter; forgiveness makes us better. Forgiveness makes it possible to move past the past. Dwelling in the past is miserable. I don't want to stay there.

Grief is a complex mixture of many things, and anger is part of the mix. To find healing, anger must be faced and confronted no matter how unpleasant it might be. Many grievers have highly justifiable reasons for being angry—angry at what happened, angry with people who were at fault, and angry with God because we can't comprehend why He allowed something like that to happen. Anger is poisonous if we don't come to terms with it. Unresolved anger is often the biggest roadblock to our ability to sense God's presence or hear or receive from Him.

If you've ever had a painful wound cleaned, medicated, stitched, and bandaged, that's what venting my anger was like. Painful, but necessary so that the wound can heal and not continue festering. Just as caring for a wound is not complete without bandaging, after my stormy fury, I met with a friend and we talked through it. She prayed with me. and we let God bandage and soothe my heart.

Anger is a legitimate emotion. It's what we do with it that makes anger health-restoring or health-destroying.

Bottled up inside, unresolved, anger festers into ever-increasing pain. Vented inappropriately, it can be destructive and damaging to ourselves and others. Once again, I turn to journaling to unlock the door and clean out the closet of my heart where anger is lurking. Talking to God and then talking with a trusted friend are healthy steps in resolving anger, coming to terms with it, and letting it go.

MILEPOST 12
POISONOUS PITY

I threw a big party and invited no one but myself. It was a doozy of a party, too. Restless, and irritated by everything, I let my sour mood seethe. Don't I have a reason? Don't I have a right to feel miserable and sorry for myself? Don't I deserve some pity? Aren't I justified in throwing a tantrum?

Pity parties are poisonous, and I was feeling mighty wretched after wallowing in that mess for a while. Finally, I cried out to God. You know what I discovered? He had attended my party. I thought I was alone, but no, He was with me the whole time. Quietly waiting. Waiting for me to notice His presence and notice that He wasn't offended by my tantrum. He held out His arms to me and gently beckoned me to come to Him.

My tears are not unseen or unfelt by a tender-hearted God. Whenever I feel alone, it's almost always because I'm too intensely wrapped up in myself to notice that I'm wrapped in His arms of love. I've never been abandoned or left alone even when I don't invite Him to my pity parties.

MILEPOST 13
FROM WRESTLING TO RESOLUTION

Then Jacob was left alone; and a Man wrestled with him until the breaking of day.... "I will not let You go unless You bless me!" (Genesis 32:24, 26 NKJV).

Genesis 32 tells of when Jacob wrestled with God, refusing to give up until God blessed him. I'm reminded of that story because I've had some wrestling matches with God lately too. Not only wrestling with God, but also with myself. Wrestling with fear, doubt, guilt, anger, depression, but more than anything, wrestling with the big questions. Sometimes in the wee hours of the morning, I'm in a wrestling match with God, and I won't give up or relent until resolution comes.

People frequently commented on the close relationship Jeanette and I had. As adults, we're more like sisters or best friends. Our relationship as a mother and daughter was truly blessed. But most people were not aware of how our relationship was forged. During her teen years, we clashed and fought like most mothers and teenage daughters. We locked wills almost daily, it seemed.

I grew up in a family where clashes like that were hardly ever resolved. Flared anger one day was ignored the next as if it had never happened. We rarely ever talked about it afterward or worked through the underlying issues. That lack of resolution was disconcerting to me, so when it came to raising my child, I determined to persist in working out problems, no matter how difficult.

During Jeanette's teen years, I doggedly followed through with my insistence to settle our differences. At times, Jeanette would lie on her bed, her back to me, facing the wall while I stood leaning against the door frame of her room, arms folded, foot tapping, the tension, anger, and frustration between us almost palpable. It was a standoff of wills, neither of us speaking, but I refused to leave until we settled matters. Struggling to find words, we'd finally speak, and soon, I'd be sitting on the edge of her bed as we tearfully, and often with laughter, sorted through the issue between us. It was our way of wrestling to resolution.

These days, my wrestling matches with God, myself, my emotions, and the big questions are mostly resolved on paper. I write. I fight. I wrestle my way to resolution, and I don't quit or give up until I'm satisfied. I don't necessarily get the answers I want, but the resolution I receive is peace, comfort, renewed faith, hope, and the grace to keep going. Must I wrestle God for these things? Is He unwilling to give me what I need unless I fight for it? No, that's not it at all. Just like the night Jacob wrestled with God or my wrestling matches with Jeanette, it's about working through my complicated thoughts and emotions until I'm able to receive the blessing God had for me all along.

Just as people often commented on the relationship between Jeanette and me, people now remark on how I'm walking through my loss with grace. But what they don't see is the conflict, the struggle, and the tears. They don't see my pre-dawn wrestling matches with God. That's where I find resolution, peace, strength, and the grace to walk this path.

MILEPOST 14
PHYSICAL SIDE EFFECTS OF GRIEF

Even though we use the words emotions and feelings interchangeably, there is a difference. One view is that feelings play out in the mind and are primarily a mental state, while emotions provoke a physical response. For example, fear might be a sense of anxiety from worrisome thoughts, or it might involve a physical fight-or-flight response. When it comes to grief, this distinction between emotions and feelings is significant. If grief is only a feeling, I should be able to exercise some self-control and get over it. Is there something wrong with me if I can't? Am I going crazy? Am I weak or lazy, or just trying to get attention? To these questions, the answer is no.

Grief is not just a feeling. In fact, grief often exhibits many physical side effects. Experts say it is like recovering from major surgery. "We should think of ourselves as a patient in intensive care and treat ourselves that way."[1] Side effects of grief may include exhaustion;

insomnia; loss of appetite or overeating; weight loss or weight gain; fogginess; inability to focus or concentrate; forgetfulness; restlessness; easily overwhelmed; general aches and pains; chest pains; shortness of breath; anxiety; panic attacks; and PTSD-like symptoms.[2] What a list! As grievers, we need to understand that experiencing some or all of these symptoms is normal. No wonder we need to treat ourselves as if we're recovering from major surgery!

Does everyone experience these symptoms? No, not everyone does. Many factors are involved in how grief affects people. That is why we're likely to run into some folks who don't understand us and may not have much sympathy for what we're going through. Their grief experience was different, and they don't understand why we're not getting past it as quickly as they did. I used to think I understood grief too. I've faced the loss of my parents and other significant people in my life, and I've grieved each loss. But when my daughter died, I discovered grief on a level unlike anything I had ever imagined or encountered before.

It's so necessary to understand that nothing is wrong with us just because we're not getting over our grief and moving on as we ourselves or other people think we should. It's okay to take as much time as we need and do what we need to do for ourselves. Recovery from major surgery requires time and rest, and so does recovery from grief.

One of the most helpful therapies for me is coloring. Whoever started the trend of adult coloring is my hero. Before coloring books for adults were popularized, I don't know if I'd have admitted to this. Doesn't it sound rather childish or silly to say I enjoy coloring books at my age? But coloring has become a recognized activity to calm and soothe stress, and I've found healing in it.

Coloring books of all sorts and styles can be found in stores these days. The best thing about it is that there's no way to do it wrong. For me, other types of arts and crafts are stressful due to intricate instructions and multiple steps, and it's more frustrating than relaxing, but coloring is "just what the doctor ordered" for me and my grief recovery.

MILEPOST 15
SOMETIMES I NEED TO STOP FIGHTING SO HARD

Be still, and know that I am God (Psalm 46:10).

I'm fighting so hard to stay afloat in a world that's gone topsy-turvy. Fighting to figure out how to go on with my life. Fighting to make things normal again. I feel like I'm fighting against the wind, and I'm exhausted!

This morning, I remembered something from my childhood, back when my tonsils were taken out. To date, it's the only time I've ever been under a general anesthesia. I remember resisting the effects during recovery and fighting to wake up. I tossed and turned and struggled, crying out as much as my sore throat would allow, "Why can't I wake up?"

A nurse gently reassured me. "Stop fighting it. As soon as the anesthesia wears off, you'll wake up naturally."

Even after all these years, the sensation of fighting to wake up is still with me. I wish I could wake up now and discover this nightmare is all a bad dream. But alas, that is not to be. I'm remembering what the nurse said. I need to stop fighting my grief like I stopped fighting that anesthesia. Fighting, resisting, kicking, and struggling against my feelings doesn't help. As terrible as it is, I have to accept what happened. I have to accept the topsy-turvy world I'm living in now. I have to accept this quagmire of emotions. It's called *grieving*, and the only way to get through it is to go through it. That's a tough pill to swallow, and I hate it, but there's no use fighting it.

It's difficult to accept life as it is rather than as I'd like it to be. But when I stop fighting, I find greater peace, comfort, and calmness. I can focus on taking one day at a time, one step at a time. There's a time and a place for fighting. Today, I need to rest.

Footsteps through the Tangled Jungles

Are you wrestling with difficult, unanswerable questions? Do you struggle with anger or self-pity? Are you weary with the burden of grief? These are all normal and natural responses to the trauma of losing one who is so dearly loved. Recovery and healing take time. Be gentle with yourself through the process. Allow yourself time to work through the tangle of emotions, but don't stay there till the jungle takes over your heart.

Accept where you are in the process. Accept each day as it comes. Don't overload yourself with demands to be further along in the healing process than you are, and do not compare yourself to other people.

Invest in a coloring book or two and some quality colored pencils, markers, or gel pens. As you color, talk to God about what's on your heart. Draw close to Him and get to know His heart for you. Mediate on these verses and journal about what they mean to you.

- "Come to me, all you who are weary and burdened, and I will give you rest" (Matthew 11:28).
- "Cast your burden on the LORD, and He shall sustain you" (Psalm 55:22 NKJV).
- "Casting all your care upon him, for He cares for you" (1 Peter 5:7 NKJV).
- "You've kept track of my every toss and turn through the sleepless nights, each tear entered in your ledger, each ache written in your book" (Psalm 56:8 MSG).

HILLS AND VALLEYS
FINDING A NEW IDENTITY AND PURPOSE

MILEPOST 16
HEALING FOR AN INTROVERT'S SOUL

Stillness is beneficial medicine for me. I've wrapped myself in a safe cocoon, gone into hibernation, and become a bit of a recluse. When I do go out, I prefer it to be on my terms—when, where, and as much or as little as I can handle. Not everyone does well in solitude, but it's what I need right now. For some people, too much alone time leads to dangerously dark places. Friends sometimes express concern about my supposed isolation, but there's a difference between isolation and solitude.

If I had to be around a lot of other people, I would go stark raving mad. On the other hand, I know people who say they would go crazy being alone as much as I am. The point is that everyone heals in their own way, and as an introvert, steeping myself in quietness leads to deep soul healing.

In our grief, we should find what works for us and do that. There's more than one pathway through grief, and no one can tell another person what's right for them. One caveat to freedom to grieve in our own way is the need to periodically evaluate if what we're doing is really working for us. It's important to remain open to the observations of trusted friends, because we sometimes don't see what they see. Is how I'm grieving helping or hurting? Am I making progress? (Keeping in mind every baby step counts.) Or am I floundering in negativity, anger, self-pity, depression, or despair? Sometimes, we need friends to help steer us in a better direction. We should allow others to be a rudder when we need a course correction.

MILEPOST 17
HOPE, IDENTITY, AND SIGNIFICANCE

My friend Linda reminded me of this one day when I was telling her how much I miss being Jeanette's mom: "Your life has significance beyond being Jeanette's mom, as awesome as that was. Simply being you is significant, and that's awesome too."

For thirty-six years, my identity was "Jeanette's mom." No matter what else I was doing or what other hats I wore, even after she was grown up, above everything else, I was "Jeanette's mom." That's me. That's who I am. At least, that's who I used to be.

I don't know who I am anymore. That's why I needed to hear these words about the significance of my life. It's a challenge to discover what defines me now. Where do I find my identity? What is significant about my life now? Why am I still here on this earth? I maintain hope that there is an answer even though I haven't discovered it yet.

Life turned upside down when Jeanette died. Forever changed. The wound is so fresh and raw now, it might be hard to believe, but life can still be filled with meaning and purpose. Wounds do heal even if the tenderness remains and the pain never completely goes away. There must be a reason why I'm still here, and I must believe that eventually I'll find a new identity and significance for my life.

Hope is my candle in the night. I consider it a quest, an adventure, and a treasure hunt to seek out who I am and what is significant about my life now.

MILEPOST 18
HOPE, PURPOSE, AND A FUTURE

"For I know the plans I have for you," declares the LORD, "plans to prosper you and not to harm you, plans to give you hope and a future" (Jeremiah 29:11).

My life revolved around Jeanette. She was the center of my world in every marvelous way. The death of any child leaves a gaping wound and an unfillable void, but losing Jeanette, my only child, is unfathomable. It's a bottomless pit—a description that doesn't even come close to measuring the depths of my loss. I wonder if I will ever recover. Most days, I don't know how I'll survive.

I feel as if I'm drowning, flailing about in deep water, desperate for something to cling to, some foothold, some handhold, something! What is the axis on which my world now turns? What will I do now that the center of my universe is gone? What is my purpose? Why am I even here?

I have long-treasured Jeremiah 29:11 as one of the most meaningful verses in the Bible to me. Jeanette claimed it as her life verse. To meditate on it now is to marvel at the providence of God. It is a lifesaver to my drowning soul. This verse assures me that there is still a plan for my life. There is still a purpose. There is hope!

I look ahead into a future I cannot see, and sometimes my view can be quite gloomy. I turn away from those thoughts to envision brighter days and a greater purpose than I have ever known before. Nothing will ever take Jeanette's place, and nothing will ever fill the void, yet I believe a new center to my world will emerge. I do not know what it will be. But I know this: God is not finished with me yet. I'm still here for a reason. That gives me something to hope for, something to cling to, and something to live for.

MILEPOST 19
WHAT IS A NEW NORMAL?

There is surely a future hope for you, and your hope will not be cut off (Proverbs 23:18).

What exactly is this "new normal" people speak of? What is it supposed to look like, and how am I supposed to find it? I feel resentful of the very fact that there is a "new normal" in my life! Why did things have to change? Why did my life have to be turned upside down and inside out? Why couldn't life go on like it did before?

Grief encompasses so much more than just missing someone. I grieve for a whole way of life that is forever gone. I miss what Jeanette and I used to do together: our fun times, our mother-daughter times, our silly texts, our teasing, her laughter, her wit, her sarcasm. I miss quoting lines from movies and guessing which movie it was from. I even miss her moods. I miss the way I used to try to make her laugh and she'd get annoyed with me. I miss our competitiveness and how both of us wanted to have the last word in an argument. My new normal is devoid of all these things and more, and that's why I resent it so much.

But I find odd things about this new normal surprising. For instance, I don't have to worry about her anymore—her health, her safety, her well-being, and happiness—these cares are like a weight that's lifted. It's strange to have exchanged the far heavier weight of grief for the smaller weight of worry. One would think I wouldn't even notice the small weight that *isn't* there because of the heaviness I carry now, but I do.

My new normal is a mishmash of many different emotions, upset routines, life adjustments, and changes I haven't even discovered yet. It's an understatement to call what's happened an upheaval. I sympathize with the dinosaurs the day after that meteor fell out of the sky. Will this new normal be the end of me, or will I adapt and learn to survive?

I can be so overwhelmed by grief that my mind can't hold another thought. Then a simple verse will come to mind, such as Proverbs 23:18, that puts life into perspective. As I struggle with the crazy hills and valleys, God assures me of hope for the future. Yes, I *will* figure out my new normal. Life *will* even out eventually. I don't have to have it all figured out right now. I just need to keep putting one foot in front of the other, one day at a time.

MILEPOST 20
MY GRIEF JOURNEY, FOUR MONTHS IN

Wrapping my mind around the fact that life will never be the same again feels simply bizarre. Some things do remain the same, and some days even seem almost normal. Except that in every little daily thing, there's no Jeanette.

It's impossible to fathom never hearing her voice or her laughter again. Never texting back and forth with her. Never going out for coffee. Never again watching TV shows and movies together and discussing them afterward. Never sharing our deep thoughts, debating our different points of view, or enjoying—a little too much sometimes—our verbal sparring matches.

So many mementos around the house remind me of her. I see her creative, artistic touch everywhere. And to think she's not here to make new things or add her special touch to anything again.

Oh, so many memories! I can barely go anywhere in this town—or in this corner of the state—without some memory of Jeanette attached to it. It's hard to imagine not going to our favorite places together again. What adventures and awesome times we had! But no more.

It's hard to imagine making new friends and trying to describe Jeanette to them when they never knew her. How will I ever explain how amazing she was? It's hard to imagine growing old without Jeanette being there at that stage of my life.

They say grief never ends, and this is exactly why. From this point on, Jeanette will never be in our lives again. For the rest of my life, I will miss her. I will learn to cope, and I'll manage to go on with my life, but it won't ever be the same.

I struggle almost every day to go about my daily life. Grief, besides being emotional, is physically taxing. I have trouble sleeping. I'm exhausted all the time. I have extremely low tolerance for frustration, and tears flow at the drop of a hat. On especially hard days, all I can manage to do is simply breathe. I have trouble concentrating. I'm forgetful. I procrastinate. I used to always be on time; I was rarely late for anything. Now I struggle to keep track of bills being paid on time.

Jeanette's death was so sudden, and the shock of it traumatized me. Now it feels as if I'm constantly waiting for the other shoe to drop. What terrible thing will happen next? I can't describe the powerless, helpless feeling of being unable to stop the next crisis. Every day. All the time. I live with this underlying fear now.

My husband expresses his grief differently than I do. I talk about it a lot more than he does. He's not ashamed of tears, but he is more private about his grief. Emotional triggers differ for us. We try to be sensitive to each other in that regard. In many ways, grief has brought us closer together and strengthened the bond between us. In the early weeks, we felt easily irritated with each other because we were both so tired and stressed, and our emotions ragged. We agreed to be gentle, recognizing how much we were both hurting and how hard this was on both of us.

Through all this, I must brag about my friends who, in my opinion, are some of the greatest friends on the planet. I've heard sad stories from others about how friends deserted them, stopped talking to them, made uncaring remarks, or judged them. I'm blessed to say that has not been my experience. Through it all, my friends have circled the wagons around me and have been supportive in so many ways. I have learned to avoid some situations and a scarce handful of people because I don't have the energy for them, but they are few. It's okay to be self-protective and make choices to maintain my peace and stability.

My perspective on many things has changed. I view some things that used to seem important as insignificant now. Other things have taken on much more prominence. For example, more than ever before, I want to make the world a better place. Well, maybe not *the* world but at least *my* world. What matters most is making a contribution that counts. If I can use this experience to somehow help someone else, it will not be in vain. What small thing can I do today to brighten someone else's day?

Footsteps over the Hills and Valleys

Call out for insight and cry aloud for understanding … look for it as for silver and search for it as for hidden treasure (Proverbs 2:3–4).

If any of you lacks wisdom, you should ask God, who gives generously to all without finding fault, and it will be given to you (James 1:5).

Reading these verses from the perspective of a griever in search of a new normal brings out how very practical they are. We weep over the changes to our lives that have been forced upon us. What choice do we have but to figure out *how* to live from this point on? For this, we need wisdom—a wisdom that is often elusive at this stage of the journey. Hence, the treasure hunt.

To view life as a quest or a treasure hunt is not only constructive, it's also a very healthy strategy in traversing the hills and valleys of grief. Some days, we find treasure right in front of us, and other days, we must dig for it. Either way, if we make it our quest to seek out alternatives for what we've lost—our purpose, our future, and our hope—the pathway of our new normal may reveal surprises.

The problem is we often either don't notice treasures in our path or we forget about treasures we've found. We need reminders. So, for this Footstep activity, you need a container. It could be anything from a Mason jar to any small box or container with a lid. Decorate it any way you like. From now on, this is your treasure chest. Begin to fill it with things that bring you comfort, joy, peace, love, hope, or things that remind you that God's not finished with you yet, and that you have a purpose and a future. You might write Bible verses, encouraging or inspirational quotes, or what you're grateful for on small notecards to put in your treasure chest. The contents of your treasure chest will be unique to you. What encourages you to keep pressing on? What brings light to your dark days? What treasures do you find that help you through your grief? On days when you have difficulty finding a treasure, go to your treasure chest for reminders of the treasures you have already found.

RUGGED TRAILS
GOD'S UNIQUE WAYS OF COMFORT

MILEPOST 21
GOD'S PRESENCE QUIETS MY FEARS

Trust in the LORD with all your heart and lean not on your own understanding (Proverbs 3:5).

In quietness and trust is your strength (Isaiah 30:15).

Since Jeanette died and my worst fear came true, I feel more vulnerable to fear than ever. Anxious thoughts stalk me as prey. What's preventing something else horrible from happening? This doesn't seem like an idle worry anymore. It raises questions about God and prayer. My trust is shaken, and I wonder if my prayers matter.

If only God prevented tragedy and sorrow from touching our lives. But that's not how life works. The paradox of good and evil in the world causes some people to be angry with God. If it's in His power to prevent evil, why doesn't He? Atheists nearly always use this argument against God. I sympathize with those who question; it's okay to question. In the struggle for answers, it's an opportunity for our faith to grow. Ultimately, it is a matter of faith and choice. I choose to believe in God, and I choose not to be angry with Him just because I don't understand everything.

Despite my fears and anxieties and even though I have questions, I've put aside doubts about God Himself. My confidence in Him has become even more unshakable, with or without answers, because I've come to know His heart. I've learned that, even when I don't understand why things happen, it's not because He failed. It's not because He doesn't answer prayer. Nor is it because I did something wrong or because Jeanette did something wrong, or any of those accusatory thoughts.

I could not survive this were it not for God's help, strength, and peace. I feel His arms of love enfolding me. I feel Him with me. I also know God loves to turn situations around. He delights in turning tragedy to triumph. That is where I find true victory. It's not about God preventing tragedy. It's about the miraculous way He turns it around and how He walks beside me through the valley of the shadow of death. Therefore, instead of clinging to my fears and my questions, I release them and let them go. I find rest in trust and confidence in God.

"The LORD is good, a refuge in times of trouble. He cares for those who trust in him" (Nahum 1:7).

MILEPOST 22
SOMETIMES BAD NEWS COMES

They will have no fear of bad news; their hearts are steadfast, trusting in the LORD (Psalm 112:7).

Bad news. News of my worst fear coming true swept into my life and turned it upside down. No warning. Blindsided. Bad news came, and fear whispered darkly, "If this can happen, then that can happen." Or if I hear someone else's bad news, fear insinuates, "If it happened to them, it could happen to you." My mind begins to extrapolate all the worst-case scenarios. That's what fear does best. Fear is a bully. Fear intimidates. Fear backs me into a corner and makes me feel weak, powerless, and helpless. Fear turns me into a victim.

Sometimes bad news comes, traumatizing you. The realization that fearful events do happen gives birth to even more fear. But fear is a bully, and how do you stop a bully from picking on you? One way is finding someone bigger to stand up to the bully and fight for you. That's God. He's our champion against fear.

The Bible doesn't say we won't ever *hear* bad news. But it does say that we will have no *fear* of bad news. Why? Because we're trusting in God. Trust keeps our hearts from being shaken. Trust is our weapon against fear. Trust enables us to fight back and not fall prey to fear's bullying.

Sometimes bad news comes. Fear points to it and says, "God failed you. God doesn't care about you. He didn't keep His promises." No! Not true! Bad news does not mean God doesn't care or failed to keep His word. The truth is, we live in a fallen world, but God didn't intend it to be that way. We have a foe who makes trouble for us. Just read Job's story. Not God but Satan wrought destruction in Job's life. But God does not leave us defenseless, helpless, and powerless. God turns the tables on that victim mentality. In trust, we find the strength to rise above it. In the end, we can say, "Take that, Satan!"

Sometimes bad news comes. Fear accuses: "It's because of this. It's because of that. It's your fault, his fault, her fault, God's fault." Trust silences the voice of the accuser. Assigning blame is not the answer. Jesus died to ransom and redeem any basis for blame (real or imagined).

Sometimes bad news comes. Fear raises a red flag of questions and waves it in our face, demanding answers, causing confusion, creating doubt. Fear shifts our focus to the unexplained, the mysteries. Trust holds us steady in the onslaught of the unknown. Trust keeps our eyes on God. He calms fear, and we find peace in the storm.

Sometimes bad news comes, and fear outright lies. "God isn't real. He's just a make-believe story." Trust laughs in the face of fear. "I know whom I have believed" (2 Timothy 1:12). "She is clothed with strength and dignity; she can laugh at the days to come" (Proverbs 31:25).

Sometimes bad news comes, but my heart is steadfast, trusting in the Lord. Not blind trust. Not flimsy, wavering, uncertain trust. Rather, rock solid. Substantial. A tower of strength. Trust smashes fear and kicks it to the curb.

MILEPOST 23
WHAT TO DO ABOUT MOTHER'S DAY AND FATHER'S DAY

God places the lonely in families (Psalm 68:6 NLT).

A pitiful vision of the future forms in my mind of Dennis and me, years from now, two old people rattling around in a house too big for us, alone, wondering what's the point of holidays. Reaching further into the future, I fear being alone in a nursing home, deserted, forgotten, with no family to visit me. It's a dismal, pathetic outlook, but these are the kinds of the fears that confront me. It makes me wonder what action I can take now to keep these fears from coming true.

First, those pessimistic pictures of a gloomy future need to be banished from my mind. I don't need that kind of negativity. Next, I need to remove holiday celebrations from the restrictive box of expectations. Mother's Day and Father's Day are the first challenging holidays we've faced since Jeanette's been gone. We're in the earliest stages of adapting and adjusting to her absence, and I'm realizing the need to broaden our definition of family. No one can take Jeanette's place, of course, or fill the void she left behind, but the compensation of friends is immense. It means the world to us when friends include us on family holidays.

If we want friends who will be there for us on special days and on into the future, we need to nurture our relationships on the ordinary days in between. We must set about intentionally building relationships. Close friendships do not spring up out of nowhere. As we invest in loving others, we face far less chance of being alone in the future.

MILEPOST 24
GOD SURROUNDS ME WITH HIS LOVE

The LORD your God in your midst, The Mighty One, will save; He will rejoice over you with gladness, He will quiet you with His love, He will rejoice over you with singing" (Zephaniah 3:17 NKJV).

It's the oddest sensation. It's as if music is being played just out of my range of hearing. If only I could tune into it like a radio station, then maybe I could make out the words. How strange to *almost* hear a song in my head but not quite. And then this verse, Zephaniah 3:17, came to mind. As difficult as it's been lately, yet some days, I'm filled with such an unbelievable sense of peace. Philippians 4:7 talks about a peace beyond our understanding. I can't explain this soothing calm any other way than as supernatural.

Sometimes, God sends me gifts, like the Jeanette cloud I wrote about in Milepost 6 or this sensation that the Holy Spirit or maybe angels are singing over me. I could easily dismiss such incidents as imagination, but no, I don't think so. God knows how hard each day can be, and He sends these special blessings to comfort me and remind me of His love. My response is to look up and say, "Thank You, God, I know that was You."

Something one person might scoff at as an overactive imagination might be very comforting to someone else. Special blessings like this are personal, and I'm not about to take that away from anyone. The adage of not raining on someone's parade is very apt here. If something comforts us, leave it at that, and please don't tell us it's silly or stupid.

These experiences are treasures to write down and keep in our treasure chest to comfort us on another day. (See previous Footstep.) God knows us so intimately that He gives us just what we need when we need it. Thank You, God, for singing over me and quieting me with Your love.

MILEPOST 25
PRESSING ON

Forgetting what is behind and straining toward what is ahead, I press on toward the goal to win the prize for which God has called me heavenward in Christ Jesus" (Philippians 3:13–14).

Forgetting what's behind? Not even possible! Nor do I want to! I understand the point, though. I can't allow myself to get stuck living in the past. I can't park here in my grief and continue looking in the rearview mirror. The strain to keep moving forward is a battle. Every day is a struggle to get out of bed and do something—maybe just one thing, but something. It might only be baby steps, but if that's all I can do, it's an accomplishment. It feels better to take one baby step than to not do anything at all.

My journey isn't over. I hear the upward call of God. I'm straining to catch a vision of new possibilities for my life. I believe in the potential of each new day. I believe there is purpose. I believe the promise. Every day, I'm moving Heavenward and closer to a joyous reunion with Jeanette. But what about *this* day? How can I press onward today? What one thing of value can I do while I'm on this journey toward Heaven?

Footsteps over Rough Terrain

A great source of comfort when the road is rough is to meditate on the names of God in the Bible. His character, His attributes, and His nature are reflected in His name. Mediating on who God is for us in our grief will strengthen our relationship with Him.

- He is *Abba* Father. We are His children. Picture Father God holding us in His loving arms as a father holds a child. Oh, how I need that some days.
- He is El Roi, the God Who Sees. I'm so thankful He sees all that we're going through: our struggles, tears, fears, and all.
- He is Jehovah—I AM. He is everything and whatever we need.
- He is Jehovah-Raah—The Lord is our Shepherd, whether we're walking in a meadow or in the darkest shadows. He is with us, caring for us, and providing for us. He is also our strong tower and refuge.
- He is Jehovah-Shalom, our peace. Jesus is called our Prince of Peace. Though our lives are filled with turbulence, in Him, we find shelter, rest, and a respite from the storm.

I'm only listing a few of His names. I encourage you to study the names of God and learn more about them. Journal about what they reveal about His nature and what it means for us as we walk the rugged roads of our grief.

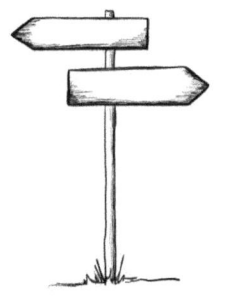

SCENIC OVERLOOKS
WHAT CAN I SEE FROM HERE?

MILEPOST 26
PERMISSION TO ENJOY THINGS AGAIN

Memories bring a fresh stab of sorrow. A sight, a sound, or a smell can rouse a memory at any moment and reopen the wound. I wonder if I will ever find enjoyment in the same activities again. Activities that used to bring happiness. Activities that used to make me laugh. Activities I used to call good times. But now they remind me that I'll never enjoy those activities with Jeanette again. I miss her so much!

And yet, I am learning healing comes through giving myself permission to enjoy some of those activities again. It's not the same, of course. It can't be, and it won't be. But I'm open to the possibility that *maybe* I can still enjoy some of our favorite activities in a new way. Even though it hurts—sometimes, it hurts a lot—I'm finding, little by little, I can do a few activities we used to enjoy together. I tell myself it's not a betrayal to enjoy these things without her. In fact, I'm sure she would want me to enjoy them. I like to think she's watching over me as I go to our familiar places or eat foods we used to love or laugh at silly movies, and I'd like to think she is enjoying each activity with me from her vantage point in Heaven.

It's complicated, this mixture of sadness and happiness. Taking small steps is part of the healing process, so I attempt small steps whenever I can. Zechariah 4:10 tells us not to despise small beginnings or small steps. Every time I do something difficult, it's a beginning, and even taking baby steps is a move in a positive direction.

MILEPOST 27
REFLECTIONS ON OLD AND NEW

Make new friends, but keep the old, one is silver and the other gold. – Patricia Connelly, et. al.[3]

Jeanette's troop used to sing this song many years ago when she was in Girl Scouts. These days, it would be relevant to my life to change the word *friends* to *memories*, and sing, "make new memories, but keep the old."

I went for a drive today to get out of the house and get some fresh air. I couldn't help but think of all the places in the area with memories of Jeanette. We've lived here more than twenty years—two decades of going places and doing things—so it's hard to go *anywhere* that we haven't been to together. How many times have I driven these roads, viewed these mountains, and traversed this valley with Jeanette? I'm thankful for so many excellent memories, but it's awfully hard to travel the same roads and see the same sights without her in the car beside me.

Today's excursion, which was supposed to cheer me up, made me more melancholy than ever. Then that old Girl Scout song came to mind, which actually made me chuckle a bit. It's terribly sad not to be able to make new memories with Jeanette and to know that my memories from this point on will be without her. Nevertheless, I can build on the foundation of our happy times and memories. Haven't I already begun to do that? And aren't the new memories worthwhile and valuable too?

The underlying fear is that new memories will replace the old ones or that new memories will somehow infringe on the old ones. But seriously, that won't happen. Doing things without her will not diminish cherished memories with her. I can keep all the wonderful memories of her *and* make new ones too. My memories with Jeanette are not threatened by new memories without her.

MILEPOST 28
THE MENTION OF HER NAME

When I held Jeanette as a newborn baby, I marveled that a new life had come into the world—a life filled with promise, a life unique as her fingerprints, a life that wasn't here before. These days, the song from *The Lion King* about the circle of life comes to mind. Jeanette was born many years before the movie, yet the circle of life summarized my thoughts as I held her in my arms. Such an overwhelming thought to contemplate. Generations past and generations yet to come, and here she was, taking her place in the grand design of life.

That's why the mention of her name now is more to me than just a memory. Her name is the essence of who she was: all her uniqueness, her gifts, her personality, her outlook, her presence, her smile, her laughter, her heart, and more. I will speak her name often, and every time I say it, Jeanette and her legacy are honored. She lives on in the mention of her name.

The thirty-six years of her life passed like a vapor, here and gone in a flash. Like the incoming tide washing away footprints in the sand, time will eventually wash away her memory. But not yet. Not! Yet! At least as long as I am alive, she will be remembered. If nothing else, I live to be a place holder, keeping her place, and carrying on her legacy. She was *here*, and her life mattered!

MILEPOST 29
AT THE SIX-MONTH MILEPOST

Looking back to the day Jeanette died is like looking through the wrong end of a telescope. It feels much, much longer than six months. It's as if an earthquake has obliterated our world, and there's no way to go back to what was.

The reality of it is undeniable, and yet the strangest, oddest sense of unreality permeates every day. I'm still wondering, as I did that day in ER, how such a thing could have happened. I still can't wrap my mind around it. Reality seems out of sync. Try as I might, I cannot get life back into alignment.

As we mark the six-month milepost, Dennis and I are both experiencing more emotions. Tears come easily. Her absence leaves such a huge chasm in our lives. It hurts beyond words. And yet, we have learned that our lives can go on. It's no longer a question of whether we can survive; we know we will.

We took the hardest hit we could possibly take. It knocked the wind out of us, but it didn't keep us down. We can laugh in spite of tears. We can look toward the future with some measure of hope. We are moving forward inch by inch. One day at a time, we are putting one foot in front of the other. But it's the hardest thing we have ever done or ever will do. My biggest and most important motivation is wanting Jeanette to be proud of me. Jeanette was a gift to me. Getting up, going on, and living my life as fully as I can is my gift to her.

MILEPOST 30
BUILDING BRIDGES ON THE JOURNEY

I didn't choose this journey. This rugged path, with steep up-and-down hills, deep shadows one day and scorching sun the next, is a solitary journey. My path is my path, and no one can walk it for me, and no one else's path is exactly like mine. Even so, as I meet other bereaved mothers, we link arms and walk together on our journeys because we have an insider's understanding of what we're all going through. What a blessing it can be to share the stories of our journey.

In the movie, *Shadowlands*, C. S. Lewis says, "We read to know we are not alone."[4] I love that quote for many reasons. Now it's why I write. I write to know I'm not alone and so others will know they're not alone either. I write for all my fellow travelers, traipsing along this lonely and weary road called grief. I am a bridge-builder, building bridges to help us over the rough places, crossing the voids of darkness, connecting us with hope and light, and navigating us to smoother roads ahead.

My footstep for today is to share what I'm writing with someone else. It's not right to keep my thoughts in a notebook or store it on a flash drive without anyone else ever reading it. Why build a bridge if it doesn't connect to anyone? I shouldn't be afraid to let other people join me on the journey.

Footsteps that Measure Progress

When people think of Arizona, usually cactus and high temperatures, not mountains, come to mind. People are often surprised to learn how mountainous the state is. When we first moved to Arizona, mountain roads, with their drop-off edges and deep, downward views scared me, but now that I'm used to them, I can drive these roads, admiring the view, not fearing for my life.

I love it when I can take the time to stop at a scenic overlook. One of the most awesome sights is the view: the expansive valleys; foothills; hazy blueish mountain ranges in the distance; and the twisty, winding road we just traveled on. It reminds me of grief when we've been laboring on the upward climb, too consumed with our efforts to notice how much ground we've gained. When we take a moment to look around and see the broader, bigger picture, we may be amazed.

Wouldn't it be nice to stop at a scenic overlook and see how far we've come on our grief journey? Our scenic overlooks are figurative, of course. Instead, one of our best means of measuring our progress comes through journaling. We're not likely to notice a major difference in the short term, but over time—three months, six months, a year—it's amazing how much we can see when we look back at what we've written.

Not everyone is a writer, but the good news is journaling doesn't require you to be. Silence the inner voice of your schoolteachers, because there's no one to fuss over spelling, punctuation, grammar, or even neatness, nor does journaling even require complete sentences. You don't need a fancy journal or notebook, but if you want one, stores offer many choices of styles and colors. Most of the time, I write in an ordinary spiral notebook or on notebook paper in a three-ring binder. Handwriting is the most effective method of journaling. It engages the brain, the senses, the mind, and emotions in a way that typing on the computer or electronic device does not.[5] But no matter how you journal, just begin, and you'll soon discover how beneficial it can be.

You might wonder what to write about. Where do you start? You can begin by just writing about what's on your mind. What are you thinking about? How do you feel today? What's on your to-do list? What would you rather be doing? Is there a Scripture on your mind today or something encouraging you've read or viewed? What are your thoughts or feelings about it? What is God speaking to you? What would you like to talk to God about? What memories are on your mind? What would you say to your child if you could talk to them?

These questions are good for priming the pump to get you started. Pretty soon, more ideas will come to mind. Develop a regular habit of journaling—if not every day, aim for once or twice a week. It's amazing how much it helps in grief and aids us in sorting through our complex and deep emotions.

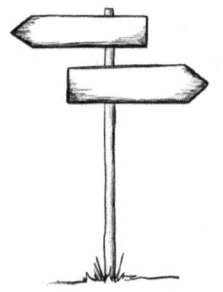

ARE WE THERE YET?
EXAMINING BELIEFS ABOUT HEAVEN

MILEPOST 31
MILES TO GO BEFORE I SLEEP

The woods are lovely, dark and deep,
But I have promises to keep,
And miles to go before I sleep,
And miles to go before I sleep.
"Stopping by Woods on a Snowy Evening" – Robert Frost[6]

Robert Frost is one of my favorite poets. Like many other fans, I love his poem, "The Road Not Taken." The elegant simplicity of "The Pasture" makes it a favorite of mine too. I well remember "Stopping by Woods on a Snowy Evening" from my American Literature class in high school. As a fifteen-year-old, I thought it was just a descriptive poem about winter. Now that I'm older, I have the perspective to recognize the themes of life and death that my teacher wanted us to recognize in the poem, and I relate to the lament of having "miles to go before I sleep."

I talk often about finding new purpose and blazing new paths for my feet, but the reality is, I feel as if my life is in limbo. I'm unsure and uncertain of what to do or what the next step is. Even if I knew what to do, I'm not sure if I'd be ready or willing to do it. So I need all the encouragement I can find, which includes this poem. It bids me to pause for a moment, if I must, but warns me not to stop. Keep going! There's more life ahead!

Time might have no meaning to Jeanette in Heaven, but the tedious days pass slowly from my perspective. I remind myself to have patience. The time of our reunion will come soon enough. I must continue my journey a while longer for "I have promises to keep, and miles to go before I sleep."

MILEPOST 32
HEAVEN IS FOR REAL

When Todd Burpo, author of *Heaven is For Real*, (the story of his four-year-old son's visit to Heaven while undergoing surgery) spoke in Tucson, Arizona, in September 2014, Dennis and I were privileged to attend.[7] As we walked into the conference room and found seats, I wasn't sure what to expect. Dennis and I had seen the movie based on the book a few months earlier, and I was curious to hear more about Colton and the Burpo family's story. But more than that, I was seeking reassurance about Heaven as a real place. I wanted to know more about where Jeanette is and what her life is like now.

If Jeanette had simply moved to another country, I wouldn't have to imagine her life or her day-to-day activities. I could talk to other people who have been there. I could see pictures of it, Google it, and learn practically everything there is to know about it. But Heaven? What can we really know? Now that Jeanette is there, knowing about Heaven is personal. It's more than a matter of faith or belief. My *daughter* is there, and my longing to know more about where she is comes from deep in my heart. Along with all the other fears I deal with now is the fear of never seeing her again. Even though I know better in my head, my heart needed a boost. That's why hearing what Todd Burpo had to say about Heaven was so important.

As soon as he began to speak, he addressed exactly what we most needed to hear, reassuring us of the reality of Heaven and what a splendid place it is for Jeanette to be. As he spoke, peace settled over my heart. My spirit witnessed the validity of his story as he proceeded to share about his son and his family's experience and how we can be confident that his story is true. During his closing prayer, he prayed for all of us experiencing the heartache of grief, and I felt as if he was praying just for me.

Afterward, we stood in a long line to meet him. As I waited, I mentally rehearsed what I wanted to say, but when my turn came, I barely spoke two sentences. Typical. That is so me. But I had already received the most important gift from him: reassurance and hope. My heart felt satisfied and my soul at rest. Yes, Heaven *is* for real, and Jeanette is waiting there for me.

Jesus said we should store up treasures in Heaven, not on earth. "For where your treasure is, there your heart will be also" (Matthew 6:21). I understand the context of Jesus's words, but now I have a different kind of treasure in Heaven: Jeanette. God knows my heart. He understands my longing for Jeanette, and He's not jealous of how much I want to see my daughter.

MILEPOST 33
MY CONCEPT OF HEAVEN AND HOW IT'S CHANGED

While performing the mundane task of washing dishes one morning, my mind was centered on Jeanette. I wondered what she was doing in Heaven right that minute. Probably not washing dishes. Suddenly, I was overwhelmed by thoughts of the gulf that now separated us. I stood in the kitchen and wept in anguish over the emptiness in my heart and my longing for her. I asked God if Jeanette ever thought about me anymore. Had she forgotten me and the people here on earth who love her? Could she look down from Heaven and see us? Could she hear me when I talked to her? In my deep grief, all I could sense was the great void of her absence. I felt such terrible emptiness at being cut off and separated from her.

In the past, when a loved one passed away, such as an elderly person who had lived a long life and was suffering from age-related illnesses or dementia, I could easily imagine them rejoicing in Heaven—youthful, ageless, healthy, and whole. Sad as I might be to part with them, I could rejoice in their release from a body wracked by sickness and pain. Beyond that, I didn't really think much about what Heaven was like for them. But when Jeanette died, none of my previous thoughts or ideas about Heaven were sufficient. I had to know more!

I began reading books about Heaven, looking up Scriptures, and building my knowledge and concepts about it as a real place. In *The Last Battle*, C. S. Lewis called this world the Shadow-Lands because it's merely a shadow of the real world where God dwells.[8] The natural world around us is a mere copy of things in Heaven, so the world of Heaven is presumably filled with many familiar things, only they are far superior and perfect.

I'm pretty sure far more varieties of what we have on earth are in Heaven—amazing and astonishing things—more beautiful, more colorful, more alive, and of course, perfection itself. I believe Heaven has more colors than our eyes can see on earth and music will be even richer and sweeter. I wonder if, perhaps, the scale will even have more notes than what we are aware of.

I believe people will go on developing their gifts, talents, and skills, and some will discover gifts and talents they never even knew they had. Artists and craftsmen will create great works, musicians will produce masterpieces, inventors and engineers will invent and build marvels, scientists will continue making astonishing discoveries about the universe, and Heaven will still need teachers. Above all, we will never reach the end of knowing all there is to know about God.

Since God's love and presence is in everything and everywhere, it is a place of perfect love, joy, and laughter.

It's a delight to love and worship God. Worship is spontaneous and as natural as breathing. No guilt, no condemnation, no shame, no lack, and no sense of not measuring up or not being good enough exists in Heaven. Imagine living in such total love, acceptance, and peace unlike anything we've ever experienced in this life.

I also think about Jeanette as part of the "great cloud of witnesses" mentioned in Hebrews 12:1. I believe she does know what is happening in our lives, and along with Jesus, she intercedes for God's will to be done in our lives "on earth as it is in Heaven" (Matthew 6:10). From her Heavenly perspective, she is aware of things and has a clearer understanding of God's purpose and plans beyond what I can know. I believe God allows her to hear when I talk to her, at least sometimes, especially when it comes from the depths of my heart. Whenever I cry or express my sadness and sorrow, my grief is translated to her as love. These beliefs help me feel less cut off and separated from her. I find comfort in our eternal connection, a bond that cannot be broken even by death.

As a bereaved mother, my need to know about Heaven runs deep. My thoughts about Heaven are personally meaningful and comforting to me, but that doesn't mean my view is absolute or perfect. Admittedly, I do use my imagination to picture the world where Jeanette is, but I think God gives us permission because, whatever we imagine, reality is even better. Likewise, nothing I think or imagine can take away from the reality of what a wonder Heaven will be! First Corinthians 2:9 says, "Eye has not seen, nor ear heard, nor have entered into the heart of man the things God has prepared for those who love Him" (NKJV).

The apostle Paul wrote about our longing for heaven in 2 Corinthians 5:1–9:

We know that when these bodies of ours are taken down like tents and folded away, they will be replaced by resurrection bodies in heaven—God-made, not handmade—and we'll never have to relocate our "tents" again. Sometimes we can hardly wait to move—and so we cry out in frustration. Compared to what's coming, living conditions around here seem like a stopover in an unfurnished shack, and we're tired of it! We've been given a glimpse of the real thing, our true home, our resurrection bodies! The Spirit of God whets our appetite by giving us a taste of what's ahead. He puts a little of heaven in our hearts so that we'll never settle for less. That's why we live with such good cheer. You won't see us drooping our heads or dragging our feet! Cramped conditions here don't get us down. They only remind us of the spacious living conditions ahead. It's what we trust in but don't yet see that keeps us going. Do you suppose a few ruts in the road or rocks in the path are going to stop us? When the time comes, we'll be plenty ready to exchange exile for homecoming. But neither exile nor homecoming is the main thing. Cheerfully pleasing God is the main thing, and that's what we aim to do, regardless of our conditions (MSG).

MILEPOST 34
LIVING IN A WORLD WITHOUT HER

I don't like it! I don't like it the least little bit! I do *not* like living in a world without Jeanette! Allow me the luxury of stomping my foot, shaking my fist, and throwing a temper tantrum, and yes, even an ugly, nasty pity party. The world is a cold and empty place without her.

Living in a world without Jeanette is difficult beyond words. I worry about things I never used to worry about. I'm tired, moody, and cranky. I have so many more aches and pains. I'm so disorganized that I can't function. I accomplish next to nothing even though I have all the time in the world to complete tasks. Hasn't it been long enough? Shouldn't I have a grip on life by now? How long does this dysfunction last? Will I ever get over it?

I confess, at times, I can be so overwhelmed with sorrow missing Jeanette so much, and it's such a terrible heartache, that I feel *angry* when I think about how much she's enjoying herself in Heaven. I know that might not make sense, but *how dare she* be partying and having a great time up there when I'm so miserable down here! *It's not fair!*

Forgive me for my outburst. Grief is weird sometimes. One minute, I'm encouraged by a happy thought, and the next minute, that same happy thought makes me mad. It's all part of the *craziness* of grief. Although I have many satisfying and positive days, I'm annoyed when I end up in the swampland of despair again. I am overwhelmed because I miss her so much. I don't know if I'll ever become used to living in a world without her.

Today, this is the face of my grief. It's not pretty, but some days, there's just no glossing over the down-in-the-dirt battles with sadness and self-pity. I'm reminding myself that it's okay to *not* be okay all the time. It's okay if all I can do today is breathe.

Breathe in peace, exhale frustration. Breathe in calm, exhale stress. Breathe in God's presence, exhale loneliness. Breathe in comfort, exhale sadness. Just breathe.

MILEPOST 35
HOPE OF HEAVEN

He will wipe every tear from their eyes. There will be no more death or mourning or crying or pain (Revelation 21:4).

Knowing Jeanette is in Heaven is one of my greatest sources of comfort. Thinking of her rejoicing, happy, completely at peace, and totally free from pain and sorrow brings relief to my memories of her struggles here in this life. But today I'm thinking about parents who aren't certain if their child is in Heaven. They don't know if a joyful reunion with their child is in the future. What if they aren't sure if their child accepted Christ before they died? The stigmas that still exist about how someone died, such as, suicide, for example, can also bring great pain. The hope of Heaven may be clouded by these questions, and parents may bear even more heartache because of it.

It's very important to remember that no one knows your child's heart like God does—no one but God! None of us can say what might have transpired between God and another person, even in their final moments. Jesus said to the thief on the cross next to Him, "Today you will be with me in paradise" (Luke 23:43). Salvation is not based on saying a certain prayer or doing certain things. The thief had no time to mend his ways or change his behavior, but Jesus assured him he would be in Heaven based solely on his last-minute change of heart. That was all it took. Don't discount the possibility of a change of heart, which no other person is privy to. Even to their final breath, God is "not wanting anyone to perish, but everyone to come to repentance" (2 Peter 3:9). Hold on to this hope.

Footsteps Toward Heaven

In the previous Milepost, I offered reassurance about knowing whether your child is in Heaven. I'm wondering if, perhaps, you may need some reassurance about going to Heaven too. Here's what Romans 10:5–10 says:

> *For Moses writes that the law's way of making a person right with God requires obedience to all of its commands. But faith's way of getting right with God says, "Don't say in your heart, 'Who will go up to heaven?' (to bring Christ down to earth). And don't say, 'Who will go down to the place of the dead?' (to bring Christ back to life again)." In fact, it says, "The message is very close at hand; it is on your lips and in your heart." And that message is the very message about faith that we preach: If you openly declare that Jesus is Lord and believe in your heart that God raised him from the dead, you will be saved. For it is by believing in your heart that you are made right with God, and it is by openly declaring your faith that you are saved (MSG).*

Basically, this passage is talking about how salvation used to be based on keeping the Ten Commandments and the law of Moses, but when Jesus came, He fulfilled the law and brought us a new means of salvation through faith in Him. Salvation isn't difficult, far off, or something we have to work for or figure out how to get. It's believing and affirming with our words and in our life that Jesus is Who He says He is, that He died for our sins, paid the full price for sin once for all, that He rose from the dead, and now our salvation and righteousness are based on Him and His work, not in our own efforts to try and save ourselves. (See also Ephesians 2:1–9.)

Salvation is so much more than admission into Heaven when we die. Faith in Christ opens the door to a relationship that gives us the strength and grace we need to live life every single day. And oh, how we need His help to endure the loss of our child! We may face all kinds of traumas and tragedies, but He enables us to overcome, no matter what happens.

To learn more about having a relationship with God, you can connect with people in your community who teach salvation based on what Jesus did for us through His death, burial, and resurrection. Fellowship with other believers is vital for growth. That way, you can learn more about who God is and how to live life the best way possible and continue moving forward in faith. Connecting with other believers will also bring more avenues for help and comfort as you travel your grief journey. I pray that you will find a place of worship that's just right for you.

STEEP TERRAIN
ENCOUNTERING BIRTHDAYS, HOLIDAYS, AND HER HEAVEN-GOING ANNIVERSARY

MILEPOST 36
OUR FIRST THANKSGIVING IN A NEW WORLD

A verse in Hebrews references "strangers and pilgrims in this earth" (Hebrews 11:13). That's how I feel on this journey through grief. I am a stranger to this path of grief and a pilgrim on this journey in a new world. Everything I'm encountering is new and different, including all the firsts. The months from November to February are loaded with firsts that are each an emotional landmine: November birthdays for my husband and me, then the long holiday season, Jeanette's birthday, and, finally, the first anniversary of her Heaven-going in February. So the question looms over me like a specter: *How will I ever manage to get through this time of year?*

I'm a planner. My sense of security in any stressful situation comes from developing a solid plan of action with everything spelled out, every *i* dotted and every *t* crossed. There's no way I'm entering this holiday season unprepared. Truth be told, I started planning back in June, even though it's kind of hard to plan for Thanksgiving and Christmas during the lemonade and sun-tanning days of summer. The holidays are the farthest things from anyone else's thoughts, but I could already feel the panic swirling around inside. *What will we do?*

I decided one of the first things to change was the plan of a big turkey dinner for Thanksgiving. All that fuss in the kitchen for only the two of us? Ditch that idea! And I certainly wouldn't be up to inviting guests. I think I'd rather be away from home. I wanted to do something so amazing that our minds would focus on that instead of on what (and *who*) we were missing. So we decided to splurge on something special, something completely different, and something we'd never done before.

Most people probably think we went on a cruise, because that's a popular getaway these days. But no, that was not for us. We love scenic train rides. Since we live in Arizona, we also love Grand Canyon National Park. The Grand Canyon Railway scenic train from Williams, Arizona, to the Grand Canyon suited us perfectly. Maybe that wouldn't be someone else's top choice for Thanksgiving, but it was the right prescription for us. We even splurged on first class tickets, and it was worth every dime we spent. We had a truly amazing time. The train ride was great fun with musical entertainment and an Old West train robbery reenactment. In addition, we didn't miss out on Thanksgiving dinner because the hotel buffet featured a delicious turkey dinner with all the traditional side dishes.

Not that any of those things made us forget Jeanette. As if that were possible. We shed tears more than once, but it was better than sitting at home and missing her.

We filled our minds with an entirely new experience, which did help lessen the sting a little. I don't know what we'll do next year, but this was a successful first Thanksgiving. Along with planning ahead, I made up my mind to get through it by honoring Jeanette with a thankful heart—thankful for all the great times and wonderful memories, and thankful for the miracle that we're surviving in this new world without her.

MILEPOST 37
ONE CHRISTMAS AT A TIME

December—a veritable obstacle course of emotional hurdles and landmines, never knowing when the next ambush will strike. We made it through November, and now we're plowing through December.

Jeanette and I accumulated large collections of Christmas decorations. Between the two of us, I counted a dozen Rubbermaid tubs plus three large Christmas trees. Sorting through these decorations is the hardest thing I've faced all year. The tears flow freely as I unpack her snowman collection, her angel collection, her miniature Christmas trees, our Christmas stockings, and so much more. I unpack ornaments she made in first grade, in Girl Scouts, and all the way up to last year. I don't know how I'm going to get through December. The sight of these decorations is taking a wrecking ball to my heart.

Jeanette loved crafts and enjoyed making and decorating her own ornaments. Three ornaments, marked with a hand-painted 2013, will forever represent her last

Christmas with us. The sight of these sentimental ornaments, each with their own memory, releases a fresh flow of tears. The same sense of disbelief I felt in the early months after Jeanette's passing has returned. The severed timeline of our lives, forever dividing *before* and *after*, stares at me from every Christmas ornament. How could this have happened? How is it possible that she's not here?

Why am I torturing myself this way? Wouldn't it be easier not to put up a tree, not to open these ornament boxes, and not to deal with all these memories? No! Not doing this and not having these beloved symbols of Jeanette at Christmastime would be much worse!

We'd always decorate the tree the weekend after Thanksgiving, but this year, the Christmas tree stood naked well into December. Every ornament felt like a lead weight when I picked it up, and I just couldn't make myself do it. The Christmas tree was finally decorated by my best friend, Linda. While we munched on Christmas cookies, drank spice tea, and I reminisced about Christmases with Jeanette, she decorated the entire tree for me.

How do we get through this Christmas, let alone *all* the Christmases to come? As we travel forward, I don't know how we'll survive. But I am determined to raise Christmas from the ashes of our sadness. The Child whose birth we celebrate came into a dark world to be the light and to bring peace and hope. Oh, how we need *light* and *hope!* As with every other day of the year, we continue putting one foot in front of the other, one day at a time, one Christmas at a time.

"The people walking in darkness have seen a great light; on those living in the land of deep darkness a light has dawned ... For to us a child is born, to us a son is given, and the government will be on his shoulders. And he will be called Wonderful Counselor, Mighty God, Everlasting Father, Prince of Peace" (Isaiah 9:2, 6).

MILEPOST 38
MILEPOSTS AND TOLL ROADS

Dear friend, I pray that you may enjoy good health and that all may go well with you, even as your soul is getting along well (3 John 1:2).

Thirty-seven years ago, during a Kentucky snowstorm, Dennis drove me to the hospital at Fort Campbell to give birth to our precious baby girl. After only a few hours of labor, we welcomed Jeanette into the world. We named her Jeanette because it means "God's gracious gift." Indeed, she was more than a gift; she was a treasure!

Today is Jeanette's birthday—her first birthday since her Heaven-going. I wanted to plan something special to honor this day, but instead I'm sick with pneumonia. I've never had pneumonia before in my life, and I don't think the timing of this sickness is a coincidence.

The pathway of grief is a toll road. This time of year, major mileposts merge into a long stretch of tolls. Following fast on the heels of the holidays comes her birthday and next the anniversary of her Heaven-going. My body is depleted from having little to no recovery time between each milepost. I bear the brunt of it physically. Passing the milepost for her birthday exacts a high toll, and my body pays it.

Even back in the day when John penned the words of 3 John 1:2, the connection between physical health and the soul (emotions) was known. It's difficult to maintain good physical health when we're carrying such a huge emotional burden as grief. All prayers for physical healing should, in my opinion, include prayer for emotional and spiritual health and well-being because they are so often intertwined.

Taking adequate care of myself is a major challenge on this journey. The pressure to eat right, cook healthy meals, and get adequate rest and exercise adds more stress and more chores that I have little energy for. I know, of course, I'll keep paying high physical tolls if I don't take care of myself. It's an on-going battle.

MILEPOST 39
THAT DAY

The thought of my suffering ... is bitter beyond words. I will never forget this awful time, as I grieve over my loss. Yet I still dare to hope when I remember this: The faithful love of the LORD never ends. His mercies never cease. Great is his faithfulness; his mercies begin afresh each morning. I say to myself, "... I will hope in him!" (Lamentations 3:19–24 NLT).

I tiptoe into February, hoping to skirt around That Day. Avoid it. Sneak past it as if it weren't there. You know the day I mean. *That Day*, February 9, the day Jeanette stepped from this world into Heaven. The day our lives turned upside down, and grief, such as we had never known before, moved in. I try not to recall or dwell on the details of That Day even though it is stamped in my heart forever.

We've bravely traveled the path of grief, passing milepost after milepost. Trying to maintain hope and optimism, we've marched forward with our lives, learning to adapt, adjust, and accept what is. But as I stand in the shadow of this milepost, I don't feel brave at all. Instead, I want to build a wall thick enough to insulate me from this milepost more than any other. I don't want to even acknowledge it exists. I want to pretend it's just another day on the calendar. Pretend it has no effect on me. *As if!* Of course, pretending is no use at all.

In the shadow of this first-anniversary milepost, I weep till there are no more tears to weep, grieving deeper than I've grieved since the very first day. A tidal wave of brokenness spills from my heart. The torrent of emotions I've been holding at bay bursts through the floodgates. As the deluge of grief comes, instead of pushing it aside, I embrace it. These purging, purifying, deeply cleansing tears disinfect my wounded soul.

In the aftermath, peace settles over me. Clouds part, and the sun peeks through the thick gray clouds. Comforted, I rise and look beyond the milepost marked "That Day," the day of Jeanette's Heaven-going. We never would have chosen this grief journey, but finding ourselves on this road, we press on. Sometimes it's a desert. Other times, it's a dark and tangled jungle. I come to mileposts such as this and pay the toll, but all the while, I keep putting one foot in front of the other, moving forward. Tomorrow is another day.

MILEPOST 40
FINDING NORMAL IS LIKE SEARCHING FOR NEVER-NEVER LAND

Normal was obliterated the day Jeanette died. *Normal* ceased to exist. Stumbling, falling, getting up, and stumbling again became my new normal. Guilt. Anger. Sadness. Regret. These emotions became normal. Tears without measure, tears pouring from my soul, if not my eyes, became normal. Trying so hard to regain my balance and restart my life. Yelling in frustration at my image in the mirror, "What is wrong with you?" Agonizing over all my new character flaws. But are they character flaws or just what grief does to a person? Normal? The word has lost its meaning.

    I view the path of my grief as one looking down from the top of a mountain pass at all the twists and turns of the road I've just traveled. I checked off all the firsts of the first year and survived the emotional landmines from November to the first anniversary of her

Heaven-going in February. I didn't know what passing all those mileposts would be like until I reached them. I thought one time around would be my teacher, so facing the second round would be easier. No! Instead, all it taught me was what the first year was like. It didn't teach me what the second year, or the third year, or all the years after would be like. As I stand at the top of this mountain pass, looking back at the winding trail behind me, I wish I could see the road marked out ahead of me. Instead, the path disappears into the mist of the unknown.

How does one find normal on an uphill unknown, unfamiliar path? I keep putting one foot in front of the other and soldiering on. I will adjust. I will adapt. I will learn to cope. Like a person who has lost a limb, I'll learn to function without Jeanette. This process *is* my new normal.

Footsteps for the Hardest Days of the Year

It's just a fact. These days—birthdays, holidays, and the anniversary of our child's Heaven-going—are going to be rough. The big question on the minds of those on this journey is how on earth will we get through these difficult days? Here are some suggestions. As much as possible, plan ahead. The closer the day gets, the less energy we have for trying to think of what to do.

- Reminisce and talk about your child with someone who will cherish your memories with you.
- Light a candle and keep it lit throughout the special day.
- View photo albums, scrapbooks, or home videos. (Personally, this is too difficult for me at a time when I'm already emotional, but for others it is just what their heart craves. Be mindful of your own needs, and if special days are not the best time, set aside the photo albums.)
- Do something your child would have enjoyed.
- Go for a walk or spend some time in nature.
- A change of scenery can lift your mood. Plan an outing or a daytrip to escape for a few hours. If possible, plan a longer trip at certain times of the year, such as holidays or difficult anniversaries.
- Make a list of all your holiday traditions. Examine your list. Which traditions are keepers? Which ones can be set aside, at least for now? Brainstorm a list of new things to try. Don't change everything all at once. At the same time, don't hang on to a tradition just for the sake of tradition. It will take trial and error over the next few years after your loss to figure out what works for you.

- Start a collection of Christmas ornaments dedicated to your child.
- Set a place at the dinner table in your child's honor along with a favorite photo.
- On her birthday, a friend of mine buys herself a gift that her son might have bought for her. She tells people, "This is what my son gave me for my birthday." We understand what she means. It helps her feel like he's still part of her life.
- Have a birthday party for your child or serve cake and ice cream for dessert.
- Prepare and share their favorite food, drink, or dessert.
- Use special tableware on their birthday.
- It's also perfectly okay to just sit quietly and remember. You don't have to *do* anything.

You can memorialize your child in the following ways:

- Have a quilt or pillow made with some of their clothes.
- Have memorial jewelry made. You have many options: necklaces, lockets, charm bracelets, etc. These might include small amounts of their ashes if cremated or a lock of hair. Some jewelry can include their engraved fingerprint or something in their handwriting.
- Make a shadowbox with small personal items and pictures.
- Rock painting can be a fun way to remember your child or encourage others. Some people paint an encouraging word on rocks and leave them in places around their neighborhood or community to bless people. Do this in memory of your child.

- Give a tribute donation to a non-profit organization, school, or church in the name of your child. It could be a one-time gift or recurring each year on their birthday.
- Some parks, schools, churches, or other places in the community offer engraved bricks or a special plaque on a park bench as memorials for a donation. My sister, Mary, donated a bench engraved with her daughter's name, Joy, to her Christian school for the playground. We had a brick with Jeanette's name on it placed on a path in the Hummingbird Garden at Kartchner Caverns State Park near where we live. I enjoy going there and spending quiet time, especially when I'm missing Jeanette.
- Some people find comfort in a memorial tattoo, depending on their views. Don't do this on a whim. Your choice for a tattoo should be well-thought out and something you're sure about. If you're like me and this is completely outside the norm for you, talk to friends about where they got their tattoos. Go to a place with a stellar reputation and a comfortable atmosphere. Tattoo options might include a photograph, ultrasound, fingerprint, something handwritten by your child, a saying, or a Bible verse, as well as the more mainstream choices of their name or birthday.

There is no one-size-fits-all category of what someone will want to do. All these ideas are up to each individual, according to his or her personal preference. If these suggestions are not your cup of tea, they will hopefully generate ideas for you. Google what you want to know more about. Pinterest can also be a great source of ideas.

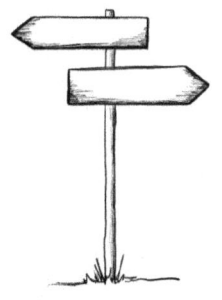

TAR PITS AND OTHER HAZARDS
ISN'T THE SECOND YEAR SUPPOSED TO BE EASIER?

MILEPOST 41
STUCK IN THE TAR PIT OF GRIEF

Grief.
Intense. Acute.
All-consuming.
As inescapable as quicksand.
No, worse!
More like a tar pit.
I'm stuck.
Helpless.
Unable to move
and sinking fast.
Too broken,
too defeated,
too discouraged
to do anything about it.

In John Bunyan's classic allegory, *Pilgrim's Progress*, the hero of the story becomes trapped in the Slough of Despond, a mucky pit of despair and hopelessness that nearly overcomes him.[9] That's where I've been lately, slogging through the Slough of Despond. It's easy to become stuck in grief, easy to make excuses for staying stuck, and easy to lose hope. I might still be there if not for supportive friends who came alongside me to help me get unstuck.

The most important thing my friends did to rescue me was to remind me that I am more than my feelings and more than appearances. I might feel weak and helpless. I might even appear to be weak and helpless. But I am not! They reminded me that I am strong in the strength of the Lord. God is mighty in me and makes me mighty. He lifts me up from the pit and out of the miry clay and sets me on solid rock. I do not have to remain in the Slough of Despond!

We may need a major paradigm shift in our thinking that moves us from weakness to strength and from being overcome to being an overcomer. We need to cease and desist from stinking thinking and think better, higher thoughts.

It's normal to get stuck in tar pits of grief sometimes, and there's no shame in it. But we don't have to stay there. When we're neck-deep in it, we may think it's impossible to get out, but that's the voice of fear and discouragement. Don't listen to the negativity. It's often much easier to escape than we realize. We just need to be shown the way. We are not alone in the pit. We are not abandoned, no matter how wretched we feel. Feelings lie to us. Reach out, reach up, and find God's hand reaching out to you. Grab hold.

"He lifted me out of the slimy pit, out of the mud and mire; he set my feet on a rock and gave me a firm place to stand" (Psalm 40:2).

"He reached down from on high and took hold of me; he drew me out of deep waters …. He makes my feet like the feet of a deer; he causes me to stand on the heights…. You provide a broad path for my feet, so that my ankles do not give way" (Psalm 18:16, 33, 36).

MILEPOST 42
VOLCANOES

A pile of used tissues and an empty Kleenex box are the remnants of my latest meltdown. I'm angry *again!* Angry because life isn't supposed to be this way. Because I don't like living without Jeanette. Because I'm alive and she's not. How the heck did *that* happen? I'm angry at death for stealing the joy out of life. Even activities that ought to be fun and times when I should be enjoying myself feel hollow and empty and pointless. I'm angry that the future looks like a long string of bleak and lonely days stretched out ahead of me. I'm angry because I want to turn back time. And I can't!

Like red-hot lava, anger came spewing from the depths of my soul this morning. The eruption has settled, and I sit here with the pile of used tissues in front of me. In the natural world, volcanoes are fearful in their destruction yet can also produce impressive results. Over the long-term, there will be fertile soil for agriculture, and miners will dig and find precious gems and minerals, thanks to the geologic process of volcanoes. Grief, though often overwhelming, can produce exceptional blessings. The potential for much value rises from the ashes. Maybe not today and maybe it will take a while, but we *will* see this devastation turn into greatness if we don't give up hope.

Keep the faith and keep believing. Keep putting one foot in front of the other. I don't care how repetitiously lame that sounds. Keep doing it anyway. One day, we'll see it was worth it.

"Be strong and take heart, all you who hope in the Lord" (Psalm 31:24).

"'But now, Lord, what do I look for? My hope is in you'" (Psalm 39:7).

"I rise before dawn and cry for help; I have put my hope in your word" (Psalm 119:147).

"There is surely a future hope for you, and your hope will not be cut off" (Proverbs 23:18).

MILEPOST 43
STAYING BALANCED ON THE TEETER-TOTTER OF GRIEF

When you were a kid, did you ever stand on the center of a teeter-totter, trying to balance both sides and keep them level? It's one thing to balance it just right, but it's another to keep it steady. Keeping my balance so that I won't be consumed by the darkness of grief is like that.

One end of the teeter-totter is a healthy grief—deeply missing Jeanette while continuing with my life from day-to-day. On the other end of the teeter-totter is a suffocating darkness that leeches every bit of light out of me. The sadness on one end is normal, but the darkness on the other end is an abyss. I'm standing in the middle, fighting to keep my balance, fighting to keep from sliding into the abyss.

When I was a child, trying to perform this precarious balancing act on the teeter-totter, I fell off, injuring my two front teeth in the fall. It was so painful, but I was trying to prove how brave and strong I was and that I could do what the big kids were doing. Instead, I fell and got hurt. I think of this now in the context of my grief. I'm trying so hard to be brave and strong. I'm fighting to keep the teeter-totter of grief balanced so I won't slide into depression. And I'm exhausted by the battle.

What if the struggle of keeping the teeter-totter balanced is not a battle I need to be fighting? Is it like when I was a kid, and I was just trying to prove something? Am I trying so hard to be brave and strong that I'm actually hurting myself?

Maybe what I need to do is to get off the teeter-totter. What I need most is simple reassurance. I need to be told that I'm doing fine and that I'm not going to fall into the abyss, even if it feels like it. I just need to let God hold me. He's got this. He's got me. And I'm going to be okay. Grief feels horrible, and I wonder how—or even if—I'm going to make it. But God is not letting go of me. I need to trust Him. He'll get me through this.

Do ever feel as if you're fighting to keep your balance and not slide into darkness? Sometimes we need to take a deep breath and find our peace in God. Stop focusing on the darkness, and it won't feel so overwhelming. Fighting for balance on the teeter-totter of grief is not always our battle. Instead, we need to trust God to keep us balanced and find rest in Him.

MILEPOST 44
THE SERENITY PRAYER

God grant me the serenity to accept the things I cannot change, the courage to change the things I can, and the wisdom to know the difference. – Reinhold Niebuhr[10]

My deepest regret is that I couldn't protect Jeanette from dying. I should have known. I should have seen. I should have done something! Maybe it wouldn't have made a difference. Maybe I couldn't have done anything. I will never know. But I will always have this regret. I didn't know she would die.

Jeanette was my best cheerleader whenever I was discouraged. When I'd beat myself up over something, she used to say to me, "Mom, you are not responsible for what you didn't know at the time." How could she possibly have known that her own words would comfort me after her death? I am not responsible for what I didn't know would happen. It is not my fault, and she would not want me to carry this burden of guilt.

I offset my guilt by thinking of what she has gained in Heaven. I remind myself that my loss is her gain. And I think of this, too—that sooner or later, if she had lived, she would be the one grieving for us, her parents, when we die. But now she never has to experience that grief or any other. It brings me consolation to know that grief can no longer afflict her where she is. I would rather carry this grief for her than have her carry it for us.

It is quite a challenge to accept what can't be changed, and it truly takes courage to live life in the shadow of such an enormous unchangeable. Yet God does give us grace for this journey.

God, grant us Your peace through all our self-doubts, feelings of responsibility, guilt, and regrets. Grant us grace to accept the unchangeable and give us wisdom to live our lives from this point on until we meet again.

MILEPOST 45
CONVALESCING

Grief such as this is not something you just get over. You learn to cope and adjust and adapt, but you don't wake up one day and, suddenly, you're over it. I can acknowledge that in my head, but the reality of it is harder to reconcile. Here's the thing. I *want* to be over it! I repeat this like a broken record; I want my life to be normal again. I want my upside-down world to turn right-side-up. Every day, I fight to make it so. But I just can't fix it!

In the beginning of my grief journey, the wound in my heart from her passing was raw, ragged, and bleeding. I wondered not only how but *if* I could live through it. Now the wound has healed somewhat. It's not quite as raw and ragged but more of a constant dull ache. In many ways, I have made progress and come so far from where I started on this grief journey. But it's still not enough. I so wish I could get over it, move past it, and get on with my life. Shouldn't I be able to? I fight a war of shoulds: I *should* do this, I *should* be that. I should, I should, I should ... Maybe I *shouldn't* be so hard on myself!

How do I make my heart understand what my brain already knows? I'm recovering from a trauma, and I must accept that convalescing is a slow, arduous process. One of the hardest things to do while recovering is to rest. Resting doesn't necessarily mean doing nothing. It's more of a ceasing to strive and to stop fighting so hard. It takes time to pick up the pieces and to learn to live with such a massive change. Resting means accepting where I am without stressing over all the shoulds. Resting is acknowledging that *I'm doing the best I can.*

I return to the Serenity Prayer again and again. It seems to be the essence of convalescing at this stage. "God grant me the serenity to accept the things I cannot change, the courage to change the things I can, and the wisdom to know the difference."[11] The hardest thing for me right now is having "the wisdom to know the difference" and being at peace with that.

Footsteps for Escaping the Mire

What does grief feel like to you? A tar pit? A volcano? A teeter-totter? A tsunami? An earthquake? Defining our grief journey with imagery and metaphors can help us sort through our emotions and put what we're experiencing into a manageable perspective. In your journaling, think about describing your grief (or some aspect of your grief) as a metaphor. Explore it from different angles and write what your metaphor can teach you.

In Milepost 42, I included some Scriptures on hope. Doing a word search for "hope" with a Bible app can help you uncover buried gems in God's Word. Write verses you find and your thoughts about hope in your journal.

Have you ever tried art journaling? Art journaling doesn't require great artistic skill any more than writing ability is required for regular journaling. It's simply another form of creative expression with therapeutic and healing value. It can be like scrapbooking. Use multiple ways to decorate a journal page to illustrate where you are in your grief journey—sketching or doodling, using stickers or accents, gluing or decoupaging cut-outs, or using fancy lettering to write an inspirational quote, Bible verse, poem, or song lyric. The possibilities are many. Specifically, for this Footstep, create an art journaling page on the theme of hope.

TWISTS AND TURNS
DISCOVERING WHAT WORKS AND WHAT TO AVOID

MILEPOST 46
ANESTHETICS

Sometimes it feels close to panic. Grief can bring a kind of terror, not knowing how I'm going to get through it. Will I always hurt this badly? Will it ever get better? What if it doesn't? I don't think I can live with this pain for the rest of my life. I'd like to somehow separate myself from the pain of grief, put up a wall, pretend the hurt isn't there, and turn a blind eye to it.

Grief understandably leads some people to all types of addictions: alcohol, drugs, food, inappropriate relationships, sex, shopping, gambling, or any other unhealthy method of numbing the pain. Grief can take people to places they never thought they'd go. We just want the pain to stop, at least for a while. I am acquainted with the temptation to numb the pain, and I haven't always won my battles. But I've learned this in the process. Anesthetics—whatever they might be—are only temporary and, ultimately, only increase the pain, drag it on longer, complicate matters, and block healing.

If we're relying on an unhealthy coping mechanism to lessen our pain, we may need outside help to break free of it, whether that help comes from friends, a support group, a pastor, a counselor, or a mental health professional. *There is no shame in reaching out for help!* When we are overwhelmed and in over our heads, asking for help is the courageous thing to do.

James 5:16 speaks truth as well. "Confess your sins to each other and pray for each other so that you may be healed." How freeing it is to be real with friends who we trust enough and who are trustworthy enough to hear our failings with love and without judgment. Such friends must also know how to speak truth in love and guide us to a place of making healthier, wiser choices.

Our ultimate support is God. He knows us better than anyone, and there's no one more forgiving, loving, and full of mercy and compassion. He is our source of strength and grace to help us overcome both our grief and our addictions.

As counterintuitive as it might seem, I find the pathway to healing is in the pain and through the pain—accepting it, allowing myself to feel it, and channeling it in better ways. Did you know some of the greatest musical compositions and artistic masterpieces were birthed in the throes of grief? Few of us are able to do that, of course, but the point is that we can find healthy ways to vent our pain that are actually productive and meaningful. Find what works for you. Just *don't* anesthetize it, which only causes more pain in the long run.

MILEPOST 47
LETTING GO

One thing I do: Forgetting what is behind and straining toward what is ahead (Philippians 3:13).

How can a mother ever let go of her child? Not even death can sever the invisible, stronger-than-steel umbilical cord connecting mother and child. No, I will never let go of Jeanette. But there is another kind of letting go.

Letting go means coming to terms with the reality that I can't go back, no wishing it weren't so, and no magic wand to wave and change what has happened. Nothing will make life the way it used to be. I must let go of life as it was in order to rebuild a new life. But that doesn't mean letting go of Jeanette.

Life does go on, but it's dreadful to have to continue without her. It's incredibly hard to enjoy life when she's not part of it. Letting go means adapting, adjusting, and accepting all the ways life is different now. Letting go means choosing to find enjoyment in life despite her absence.

I'll never let go of Jeanette. Never! But I am working on letting go of the past, reaching for what's ahead, and attempting to live the life I have now to its fullest potential—even if it's little by little, in tiny increments, taking baby steps forward.

MILEPOST 48
THE HALF-FULL GLASS

It's over a year since Jeanette's Heaven-going, and her absence still feels surreal. If I've learned one lesson in the past year, it's this: My ability to go on with life depends on where my focus is. It truly boils down to the proverbial question: Is the glass half-empty or half-full? Is my focus on what I don't have or on what I do have?

If I am focused on the emptiness of her absence and if I can't see past the hole in my heart, I don't know what hope I have for recovery. I might as well curl up and die my own slow death. How tragic!

Or, I can turn my attention to the goodness of life, to every big and small blessing that still flows through each day. I can lift my eyes off my sadness to a wider, broader view. By purposefully seeking things that are positive and valuable, I discover treasures I might not have found otherwise. Even without Jeanette, my life is blessed. Nothing takes her place. Nothing fills the void. The emptiness without her can be a deep, dark void. But her absence doesn't dictate the value in each day. Instead, my perspective defines each day.

Victory is when carbon changes into a diamond, a pearl is formed from a grain of sand, a worm transforms into a butterfly, or when beauty rises from the ashes. Transformation is God's specialty. We are given the choice to allow God to work. We *choose* to let things remain as they are or to surrender them to God so He can transform them. But even in making the choice, God comes to our aid. His Word says that "it is God who works in you to will and to act in order to fulfill his purpose" (Philippians 2:13). Praise God for coming to our aid at every level and every step to bring transformation, even in softening our hearts to make us willing where we're unwilling. It doesn't happen overnight, but we will see victory if don't give up.

MILEPOST 49
MY GRIEF JOURNEY AT EIGHTEEN MONTHS

Life's journey is a river, and life events are regions through which the river flows. I certainly didn't see this region of grief on the map of my life, but here I am. I've been rowing through this territory without Jeanette for a year and a half. I've had to adjust my oars through a multitude of meandering turns, I've endured formidable rapids, and I've floundered through fog for seemingly endless days. For now, the waters are calm and smooth, but how long that will last is unknown.

As I scan the banks of the river, I notice how different this territory is from anywhere I've ever been before. I'm encountering a whole new way of life. My outlook is changed. Many hopes and dreams have been washed away in floods of grief to be replaced by unexpected new vistas, even though my vision is limited to the next river bend.

Throughout this uncertain journey, God's presence has been tried-and-true. He's directed me through every dangerous current and guided me around each obstacle. My faith and confidence in Him have become unshakable. He's been my ever-present help in trouble. He has comforted me, brought light to my darkness, and given me songs in the night. He has collected my tears. He's held me through fits of anger, fear, temper tantrums, pity parties, and temptations. And not once has He forsaken me. Even when my attitudes have been stinky, He's loved me through it all. In Him, I find endurance, hope, and optimism as I continue on my way.

MILEPOST 50
TRANSITION

The bottom dropped out of my life the day Jeanette died. Her death threw me into a complete tailspin that I cannot find adequate words to describe. Everything that made sense about me and my life was torn apart that day, ripped away from me in only an hour's time. How can anyone describe the devastation left in the wake of such an abrupt and sudden loss? I've been struggling to make sense of life without her ever since.

    The struggle to find new life is like clawing my way up a cliff after falling off the edge. I've managed to climb back up to the top of the cliff, and now I sit on the edge of the precipice, peering into the distant haze of peaks and valleys. The glow of a dawning sun paints the heavens and the world around me in soft light. I hear faint music carried on the freshness of a new morning. I know I'm still deep in grief, but I feel a tiny bit of emerging life, a quickening, like the coming of spring. *Hope!* It's the hope of a new day dawning.

"May the God of hope fill you with all joy and peace as you trust in him, so that you may overflow with hope by the power of the Holy Spirit" (Romans 15:13).

"This is the day the LORD has made; we will rejoice and be glad in it" (Psalm 118:24 NKJV).

Footsteps for Wayward Journeys

Before grief came to my doorstep, I had no clue how hard grief is, how vulnerable it makes us, or what a precarious and fragile place it puts us in. My guess is none of us had any idea before we wound up smack dab in the middle of it. Few of us, if any, are prepared for it. All of a sudden, we find ourselves neck deep in grief and floundering just to survive.

How my heart goes out to all grievers, who, like me, are trying to figure it out, one day at a time, one step at a time. We don't always choose the healthiest ways of coping, and then we must backtrack to get unstuck from the rut we got ourselves into in addition to our grief. Seriously consider seeking whatever level of help you need: friends, a support group, a pastor, or a mental health professional. You are not alone. You are not helpless. You are not hopeless. Even when you feel that way, it is not true. You *will* get through this. Just don't give up!

We don't see the end from the beginning, but I know Who does (Isaiah 46:10). I know the One who lifts me out of the mire and sets my feet on solid ground (Psalm 40:2). I know Who to run to for deliverance from fear and despair and troubles (Psalm 34). God doesn't play favorites (Acts 10:34). If He helps me in my grief, He will also help you. No matter how hard it is, *there's always, always, always **hope**.* When your path is too dark to see the way forward, run to the Light (John 8:12, Matthew 7:7–8).

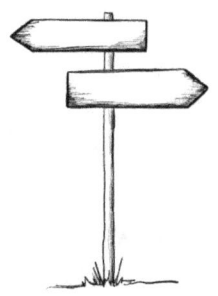

ENDURANCE TESTS
PUTTING ONE FOOT IN FRONT OF THE OTHER DAY BY DAY

MILEPOST 51
PICKING UP THE PIECES ONE BY ONE

Reconstructing my life since Jeanette's passing has been the most intense and difficult challenge I've ever faced. My life was completely disarranged, as if a million puzzle pieces had been thrown into the air, and I had to pick them up one by one. Some days, I feel strong; other days, I'm a mess. I'm my own worst critic—impatient, demanding, unrealistic—and wonder why I'm making so little progress picking up the pieces.

I most need someone to clear a space in the pile of rubble, sit down with me, and help me sort the pieces. Even my friends can sometimes feel overwhelmed by this task. But I've discovered there is One who sees the end from the beginning (Isaiah 46:10) and Who can bring order to the chaos. He is also endlessly patient and endures my meltdowns and moods du jour. He holds me, dries my tears, and shelters me in my weakness and vulnerability. He speaks grace to me and whispers,

"Don't give up hope," as He hands me the next piece of the puzzle. "Piece by piece, day by day, you're healing."

Just as I discovered therapy in coloring books, now I'm finding therapy in jigsaw puzzles. I discovered online puzzles, which is easier than having all the pieces scattered on the dining room table. But it's still the same process of sorting the pieces and finding where they fit. Oh, if only it were that easy to sort the pieces of life and put them in place. Real life is far messier and more complicated, but doing a puzzle represents hope in the process and in the ultimate reconstruction of my life.

MILEPOST 52
WHAT NO ONE EVER TOLD ME ABOUT GRIEF

"No one ever told me grief felt so like fear," C. S. Lewis wrote in *A Grief Observed*.[12] Any griever could list things no one ever told us about grief. Here's my list.

No one ever told me:

- how many myths and mistaken notions there are about grief and grieving.
- that grief is not a neat linear progression of stages—a, b, c, followed by d—but that it's a crazy roller-coaster ride of ups, downs, twists, turns, and wild loop-de-loops.
- that grief is so physical—aches, pains, fatigue, and more.
- that grief makes everything harder. Simple tasks are a chore. Frustration is multiplied a hundred times.

- how hard it can be to listen to music. I thought music would comfort me. Instead, it's often an immediate emotional trigger.
- how much grief has changed me. I'm not the person I used to be, and there's no going back.
- that grief makes me forgetful. I'd better write things down. And I'd better check to be sure I turned off the burners on the kitchen stove.
- that grief changes friendships; some are strengthened while others fade.
- that holidays and special days must be rethought, amended, and adjusted, but no matter what, the ache will still be there.
- how joy and sadness can coexist in the same moment.
- that people's expectations run the gamut from "You should be over it by now" to "I can't believe how strong you are." Neither represent reality.

We can read all the books, yet still, grief is an individual process. The path is ours to walk, and no one can walk it for us.

MILEPOST 53
SOARING ON EAGLE'S WINGS

Have you heard of the Decorah eagles? They are a pair of bald eagles viewed through a webcam above their nest near Decorah, Iowa. Every year, thousands of online fans wait in anticipation for the eggs to hatch. For the next several months, we watch as the baby eagles grow from hatchlings to juveniles and finally leave the nest.

The eagle parents care for their young with ardent devotion, bringing tasty bits of trout or squirrel for meals, fending off predators in the night, and nestling their young ones through snow, wind, and rain. Fans of the eagle family delight in each stage of growth, especially as the youngsters exercise their wings. It seems to take forever, but soon their wing muscles are strong enough to hover a few inches above the nest. Next come some of the most entertaining moments as they leapfrog over each other, hop-flying from one side of the nest to the other. Then one day, all three juveniles are in the nest, and the next, there are only two. One by one, they take flight. Even after they fledge, their parents continue training them in hunting and survival skills until they're ready to be fully independent.

As I've watched the young eagles' progress through stages of life, I can't help but compare it to my progress through the stages of grief. If only grief were as predictable. It isn't. The young eagles move from one stage of development to the next in predictable steps, but grief does not proceed from stage to stage in such a neatly defined order. The so-called stages of grief are erratic and chaotic. They are up and down, weaving in and out, backtracking and covering the same ground in repetitive cycles. Nevertheless, the cycles move in an upward progression. Even as crazy and repetitive as my progression has been, I have experienced breakthrough, growth, and forward momentum.

Growth in grief is like the young eagles as they flap their wings to strengthen their muscles for flight. The wing-flapping stage seems to last a long time. They're flapping and waving their wings, and nothing happens, nothing but wind. And then, little by little, day by day, their efforts begin to look more like something than nothing. Gradually, the young eagles work their way to their first flight. At first, they take a short hop from the nest to a nearby branch. What a day! Devoted eagle fans cheer. After that first hop out of the nest, those young eagles are soon soaring on the wind with their parents.

Grief is not a linear progression. It follows no predictable timeline like the eagles' growth, but there is a progression of growth in grief. Watching the eagles gives me hope. One day, in due time, I will soar on eagles' wings too.

Gaining strength and rebuilding life after loss takes time. It often looks like we aren't making any progress at all. We can easily become discouraged. We need to remember to be patient with ourselves, accept the stage we're in at the moment, and just keep going.

MILEPOST 54
TRUTH THAT GIVES HOPE

I find that for every truth that is difficult and tragic, there is one that is helpful and gives hope. – LaVonne Foix

One "truth that is difficult and tragic" is how quickly life can change. We begin our day with familiar routine. It seems like every other day. Until it's not. In one moment, life is changed forever. We know people this has happened to. We hear stories in the news. We hope it never happens to us. And we're afraid because it *could* happen to us despite our prayers that it won't. It's hard to know what to do with that kind of reality. Most of the time, we try not to think about it. We don't have answers. We feel a foreboding sense of helplessness and powerlessness when we think about how little control we have over events. We wonder about God. What is His role in all of this? We grapple with the mystery of it all.

But there is something quite profound in the above quote from my niece, LaVonne. When God turns things around for good—when He brings triumph from tragedy, when He lights up the darkness, when He makes the crooked places straight and the rough places smooth—He is balancing the difficult and tragic with what is helpful and gives hope.

The difficult and tragic truth in my life is my daughter's death and all the darkness, sorrow, and grief that entered my life that day. It tips the scale with a ponderous weight. How could anything balance out the scale? But I watch as hefty qualities raise the scale until it tips in the opposite direction. Hope. Faith. Trust. Resilience. Endurance. Perseverance. Courage. These qualities and more carry enormous weight. Indeed, the truth that is helpful and gives hope outweighs the truth that is difficult and tragic. I bear witness to this as one who knows firsthand. "The truth that is helpful and gives hope" makes it possible to continue onward through the darkness.

MILEPOST 55
TAPESTRY

Deep loss and sorrow are woven into the tapestry of my life. Grief changed the pattern, the thread, and the colors. But now the threads are knotted, and the tapestry is stalled in the loom. The fabric is warped and seems to threaten to break the loom in pieces. Is the tapestry ruined? What will become of it? What happens when something so life-altering occurs that the very fabric of life is never the same again?

It's difficult to see beyond my one-dimensional perspective. It's like trying to see my face without a mirror. My only view is how marred and damaged my life feels right now. If that's how I feel, it must be true, right? Or is it? Are feelings an accurate indicator of reality?

If I could see the tapestry of my life from a perspective other than this one dimension, what would I see? Could the warps and twists in the fabric be part of the design? Would I discover the knots produce a distinctive texture and the pattern and colors reveal an astonishing work of art? What if the discomfort of the loom doesn't mean that something is wrong with the tapestry? What if the tapestry of my life is a masterpiece that I'm completely unaware of?

How easy it is to forget the promise that God transforms our mess into a message. The tapestry of our lives is grand, rich, and majestic. Just because we can't see it doesn't mean it's not so. We may not be able to see it now, but we will someday. When it is finally revealed to us, I believe we will be awestruck by its magnificence. For now, may we trust the Master Weaver and allow Him to do His work.

Footsteps for the Long Haul

In "Footsteps for Trailblazing in the Wilderness," I suggested making a list of activities to give yourself a respite from your grief. That was a start, but you might have discovered more strategies since then. Have you written your ideas in your journal? Are there more strategies you can employ to push past your grief fatigue and find your second wind?

Sometimes we need to step outside ourselves, focus on others, and move our attention outward rather than doing so much introspection. Even for an introvert like me, sometimes I need to spend more time with others. Here are some suggestions:

- List three daytrips you'd like to take. Think of one to three friends who would enjoy going with you.
- List five foods or recipes you'd like to try and plan menus using them. Invite a few friends over to prepare and enjoy new or favorite foods.
- See if someone in your community does paint parties or any other type of arts and crafts group. Go to one or host one in your home.
- Start a book club with a few friends. Choose uplifting books and meet regularly to discuss them.
- Think of five friends who could use an encouraging word. Mail them a thinking-of-you card.
- Prepare a gift basket or care package for someone who could use a morale boost.
- Is there a friend you haven't seen in a while? Arrange a visit or meet for lunch to catch up.

What more can you think of?

STEPPING STONES
ROUND TWO OF HOLIDAYS, BIRTHDAYS, AND HER HEAVEN-GOING ANNIVERSARY

MILEPOST 56
BEING THANKFUL EVEN IN GRIEF

And everything I've taught you is so that the peace that is in me will be in you and will give you great confidence as you rest in me. For in this unbelieving world you will experience trouble and sorrows, but you must be courageous, for I have conquered the world (John 16:33, TPT).

We know life is not always sunny and bright. Troubles arise. But the good news is this: Jesus's victory makes victory possible for us.

I've heard people say that God will never give us more than we can handle. I'm not sure about that. I think it's more accurate to say that God will never give us more than *He* can handle. Whatever life throws at us, it's not too much for Him. and He gives us grace, strength, and whatever resource we need to handle it. That's worth some thanksgiving.

Even in this troubled world, I have much to be grateful for. I'm thankful for my relationship with God, forged over many years, teaching me that God is good, kind, loving, and trustworthy. I'm thankful that God is not distant and impersonal. He holds the brokenhearted close to His heart. I am thankful for His presence throughout every day and in the darkest night.

I'm thankful for the thirty-six years I had with Jeanette, for every memory, and for what a dear and special blessing she was. I'm thankful for the gifted teacher she was and for how many lives she touched that will never be the same. I'm thankful for her legacy, which gives me purpose in carrying it forward. I'm thankful she doesn't have seizures anymore, and she no longer suffers from sickness, pain, or heartache. I'm thankful for the reality and promise of Heaven for those who believe in Jesus.

I am even thankful for how grief, bitter as it might be, is making me a kinder, gentler, more compassionate person. I can see how I've grown in ways that I might not have otherwise. I was never aware of how many people walk this path of grief. I never knew or understood what grief is like before, so now I can help others as an insider who knows firsthand.

I believe with all my heart there is always something to be thankful for. I'm not saying I should be thankful for what happened to Jeanette or that any parent should be thankful for what happened to their child. But how truly magnificent it is that God can take a tragedy and miraculously transform it and then enable us to walk victoriously in life despite what happened. That's worth some thanksgiving.

As we prepare for another Thanksgiving without Jeanette, we can let her absence wreck the holiday, *or* we can decide to give thanks for all the blessings we still enjoy. The choice is ours.

MILEPOST 57
ACCEPTING THE BITTERSWEET

I'm listening to the theme from *Fiddler on the Roof* and thinking about the role of traditions and how they tell us who we are. At no time is that truer than during the holiday season. Everything we do during the holidays tells the story of our family, our roots, our identity, and what's important to us. That is exactly why the loss of a loved one affects the holidays so keenly. Jeanette's death changed everything about our lives but changed the holidays most of all.

We're barely on the threshold of the holiday season, but I'm already prepping my strategy for navigating the gauntlet of emotional hurdles the coming weeks bring. Every year, I resolve not to let grief rob me of the childlike wonder I've always loved about this season. I shake my fist in the face of grief and shout, "You will not steal my Christmas!" Even so, I accept that tears must come, and I allow them to flow as needed.

With all the magnificent memories I have of Christmases past, it is no wonder that it's so hard to accept that life has changed. Memories are sweet. But on the other hand, memories can serve as bitter reminders and highlight changes we did not choose or want. What else can I do but accept the bittersweet?

I always cry at the end of *Fiddler on the Roof*, but I love the story. Tradition. Identity. And change. Most of all, a poignant story of adapting to change and of enduring hope. The most predictable thing about life is that it's always changing. Some changes we choose and some we don't; whichever the case, adapting to change is a crucial life skill.

This bittersweet taste of change reminds me of the depth of my love—a love too precious to be forgotten and a love that's worth the price of grief. I accept the oddity of coexisting, conflicting emotions, bitter and sweet.

MILEPOST 58
HOPE SPRINGS ETERNAL

There is a time for everything, and a season for every activity under the heavens: a time to be born and a time to die …. He has made everything beautiful in its time. He has also set eternity in the human heart; yet no one can fathom what God has done from beginning to end (Ecclesiastes 3:1–2, 11).

Bitter can be made sweet. Beauty can arise from life's worst events. Broken things can be mended. The passage in Ecclesiastes 3:1–11 reminds us that for every negative, there's a positive, and even things that are negative can ultimately have a positive outcome. Transformation from ugliness to beauty is a promise, but it is also dependent on the choices we make.

The day my daughter died, part of me died with her. I sank into a well of darkness and might have drowned there, but that is not how I wanted the story to end. I chose life. I chose not to be bitter. I chose to see light in the darkness. I chose to allow God to transform the situation, and I discovered that He can and will. I would give anything to wake up and find that my daughter had not died. But since I cannot change that, I seek new life, new growth, new beauty, new hope, and yes, even sweetness in the bitterness of life.

God has set eternity in our hearts. This means, even though our physical lives are confined within the parameters of time with a beginning and an end, our soul and spirit are not chained within time. An eternal perspective helps us see beyond the bruises, wounds, and brokenness of our lives here. There's more to come beyond this life. All is not lost. It is not over.

The seasons of winter and spring remind us of this truth. Bare trees withstand the icy cold. Frost seems to kill everything. But then spring comes. Trees bud with new leaves. New growth rises from the once-frozen soil. God provides us with marvelous object lessons of renewal and revival through the changing seasons. Hope springs eternal.

MILEPOST 59
MAKING THE MOST OF THE DASH

A line etched into a headstone
between the dates of birth and death
represent each step we take on earth
and every breath we take. – Linda Ellis[13]

At our local hospital this morning, an elderly man breathed his final breath, while at the same time, a young woman gave birth to a beautiful baby girl. Birth and death. Two dates separated by a dash.

Life is short, we often say dismissively. Indeed. Do we realize how short? The dash between birth and death is a swift race; all the more reason to value every day. Few of us live in full appreciation of our days. We race, we run, and we try to keep up. We are driven by so many temporal things, demands, and pressures. Are we really living or merely running from one day to the next?

Making the most of every day begins with separating what is truly important from what is not. Identifying the important things in life is not that difficult: family, friends, God, love, kindness, caring for others, and so forth. What a different world it would be if we actually lived each day putting the important things first.

What would it look like if we truly made the most of the dash? For me, I think I'd notice the beautiful things around me more—from the sunrise and sunset to the shifting light and shadows of clouds passing overhead to the varying shades of blue in the sky. Or the bird songs that I need to listen to closely so that I can discern one from another. Or the small flower growing in the cracked concrete of my parking space as I hurry into the store to shop. How much time does it take to notice these simple beauties?

What if we unwrapped each day as a gift? Or what if we put down our phones or disconnected from the internet for a while? What if we attentively listened to others, hearing with our soul and spirit? If we made the most of the dash, wouldn't we do more for others, not out of obligation, but because we really care? Wouldn't we invest more in our talents and gifts while encouraging others in theirs? If we made the most of the dash, wouldn't we live life as less self-absorbed? What if we lived from our identity as a child of God so that we expressed His heart to those around us more authentically, regardless of whether they earned it or deserved it but simply because that's how God loves us? Aren't these things what making the most of the dash would look like?

Life is short even if we live to be a hundred. We can grumble our way through it. We can put on blinders and live in our own bubble. We can race to the finish line, competing for the most toys. Or we can make the world a little brighter and better because we were here, making the most of the dash every single day.

MILEPOST 60
REFLECTIONS ON THE SECOND ANNIVERSARY OF JEANETTE'S HEAVEN-GOING

In the old days, a person signified mourning by wearing black clothing or a black arm band. A time of mourning was socially acceptable. It's as if society understood something back then that we've forgotten these days. Grieving takes time, and mourners should be given space with this process.

How long does grief take? That's the big question, isn't it? Six months? A year? Two years? Is everyone else supposed to wait around for the mourning period to end? I wish there were a simple one-size-fits-all answer, but there isn't. I can only speak for myself and my journey. I'm not a poster child for everybody else's grief. Grief doesn't work like that.

Everyone grieves differently. Some throw themselves into work and activity. I cocooned myself in solitude and found my healing in rest and quiet. How does a butterfly know when it's time to shed its shell and push out from the cocoon? The time is not defined for grievers. There does seem to be a natural progression of healing, but the pattern or order is unpredictable and varies for everyone. The timeline is as individual as everything else about grief. But I can say this: A parent never "gets over" grieving a child. I've come a long way, but I have many more miles yet to walk on this journey, and it will last my lifetime.

Each new day, the sun rises and sets, and days stretch into weeks and months, and now it's been two years since Jeanette's Heaven-going. I feel as if I've climbed a mountain. I'm proud of myself for making it up this mountain for the second year, but I'm also wondering what it will be like to make this climb every single year. What will it be like to pass this milepost year after year after year? It's daunting to think of the passing years. The best I can do—and all I should do—is keep putting one foot in front of the other, one day at a time. Forgive me if I keep saying that, but I never cease to need the reminder.

Footsteps from One Year to the Next

Teach us to realize the brevity of life, so that we may grow in wisdom ... Satisfy us each morning with your unfailing love, so we may sing for joy to the end of our lives. Give us gladness in proportion to our former misery! Replace the evil years with good (Psalm 90:12, 14–15, NLT).

No one understands the "brevity of life" better than a bereaved parent. But there's more to these verses than merely acknowledging how short life is. Our prayer as bereaved parents is to see God's unfailing love, to be able to sing for joy again, to have gladness instead of our misery, and for God to replace the evil that has happened with good. These are, indeed, His promises, but we wonder when, where, and how they will be fulfilled?

Who knew emptiness could be such a heavy burden? It's hard to maintain hope that it will get better, that life can be good, or that we will ever truly feel joyful again. Faith to believe, faith that clings to hope, is crucial. Pain is real, but so is God. We're never abandoned; He never leaves us, regardless of what our feelings might say to the contrary.

Scriptures are like spiritual vitamins to revitalize our courage and hope when our strength has been depleted. Here are a few verses to encourage you.

- "The LORD is a refuge for the oppressed, a stronghold in times of trouble. Those who know your name trust in you, for you, LORD, have never forsaken those who seek you," (Psalm 9:9–10).
- "Cast your cares on the LORD and he will sustain you" (Psalm 55:22).
- "But may all who seek you rejoice and be glad in you; may those who long for your saving help

always say, "The LORD is great!" But as for me, I am poor and needy; come quickly to me, O God. You are my help and my deliverer; LORD, do not delay" (Psalm 70:4–5).
- "The LORD is trustworthy in all he promises and faithful in all he does. The LORD upholds all who fall and lifts up all who are bowed down … The LORD is near to all who call on him" (Psalm 145:13–14, 18).

How many more verses can you find about God's comfort and nearness? Be sure to record them in your journal along with what they mean to you.

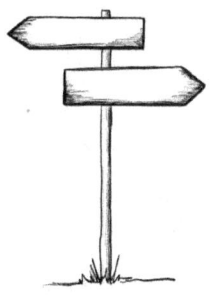

SHAKY GROUND
THE CHALLENGE OF HOLDING STEADY

MILEPOST 61
SHUTTING THE DOOR ON FEAR

For God has not given us a spirit of fear, but of power and of love and of sound mind (2 Timothy 1:7 NKJV).

Do you remember what it was like before and after 9/11? Or pick any other sudden disaster or tragedy and compare life *before* and *after*. Our sense of safety is shattered. Innocence is stripped away. Insecurities emerge and take root. Our vulnerability is revealed in stark light as we recognize how little control we have. We wonder when, not if, the next horrible event will happen. Fear takes up residence in our minds and stalks us, especially at night.

C. S. Lewis's words come to mind once again: "No one ever told me that grief felt so like fear." Fear, another element of grief, receives little attention. People don't talk about it nearly as much as sadness, loneliness, or anger. Yet fear can lead to some of the darkest places in grieving. Fighting fear is the reason I strive so hard to be positive and optimistic. Don't mistake my positivity for naivety. Don't misinterpret my faith as blindness to reality. By keeping a positive attitude, I'm digging in my heels with determination not to fall prey to fear.

Sometimes we have to be very deliberate and intentional about not letting fearful thoughts take root. We must remind ourselves of God's faithfulness and ask friends to pray with us and encourage us so that we can climb out of fear. We must also speak positively to build ourselves up in our faith. Fear might try to take up residence, but we can shut the door.

- "I sought the LORD and He heard me, and delivered me from all my fears" (Psalm 34:4 NKJV).
- "When anxiety was great within me, your consolation brought me joy" (Psalm 94:19).
- "For I am the LORD your God who takes hold of your right hand and says to you, Do not fear; I will help you" (Isaiah 41:13).

MILEPOST 62
PESKY EMOTIONS

Emotions have a mind of their own, often striking without warning. I may be going about my day's business, seemingly fine, when suddenly, *wham*! Out of nowhere, I'm blindsided by pesky emotions with no sense of propriety, ambushing me with no thought as to my surroundings. I'm caught in a public place with tears I can't control. As soon as one tear escapes, it's a lost cause holding them back. Crying is embarrassing and awkward in public. I wish I could maintain a stiff upper lip, but sometimes nothing can stop the tears. I wish my superpower were a cloak of invisibility. I don't want people to ask me what's wrong or if I'm okay. I just want to escape and pretend this never happened.

Has this ever happened to you? What do you do? How do you handle it? My first plan of action is to escape—just leave and get out of there. If that's not possible, I sometimes try to pretend I'm invisible. It works if no one is paying attention. If that fails, maybe

I can think of something clever and witty to say to lighten the moment. (But most likely, nothing clever comes to mind until hours later.) Sometimes it works to be honest and admit the truth—my daughter died, and I'm having a rough day. I'm often surprised by the compassion and kindness of others. The worst that can happen is that they stare at me blankly, not knowing how to respond. Even then, sometimes I feel better after acknowledging my grief out loud.

Any strategy for handling pesky emotions in public might work one time and not another. Just remember, it's not important what anyone else thinks. Even though we may feel awkward or embarrassed in the moment, it's not as big a deal as we think. We need to learn how to let it go and not fret about it. People's memories are short, and we can return to that store or restaurant or wherever it happened in the future, and no one will think twice about it. We should train our own memories to be short in respect to awkward moments and teach ourselves not to think twice about it either.

MILEPOST 63
I PRESS ON

For my determined purpose is that I may know Christ, that I may progressively become more deeply and intimately acquainted with Him, recognizing and understanding the wonders of His resurrection power—His ability to breathe new life into dreams I thought had died—and understanding His goodness, His grace, and His love—to grasp and comprehend His character more clearly than ever before, and that I may be transformed into His likeness more and more as I focus on His finished work in my life. With this in mind, I put yesterday behind me and I reach for what today has in store, and I keep pressing on (Philippians 3:10–14, author's paraphrase based on the Amplified Version).

Our ability to press on depends on having a determined purpose. It takes an intentional mindset to be a survivor. It doesn't happen accidentally or by chance. It's intentional.

So much hinges on our relationship with God. It's not about our knowledge *of* Him but in *knowing* Him. Becoming more deeply and intimately acquainted with God strengthens our understanding of His goodness, His grace, His love, and His character, which in turn, affects our ability to trust and have confidence in Him. Our relationship is the transformational pivot that turns our sorrow into joy and our despair to hope. It is *the* key to our ability to keep pressing on.

People commonly struggle in their relationship with God as they work through grief. Anger and bitterness need to be dealt with. We have a spiritual enemy who delights in driving a wedge between us and God. That enemy does not fight fair, and he *lies* to us. He wants our attitudes and emotions to be hostile toward God. Ultimately, he wants to rob us of our lives, but short of that, he wants us to be so miserable and filled with despair that we become victims. But we don't have to be victims. We can be victors through Christ instead.

Do not allow yourself to listen to the enemy's lies because it's like drinking poison. Do not allow your feelings to interfere with coming to God and pouring out your heart to Him. God cares about you so very much. Come to Him no matter how you're feeling or whatever state you're in. Do not let guilt, condemnation, doubts, or anything thing else hold you back. God is always ready to embrace you and love you. Press on with determined purpose to know God more and to experience more of the depths of His love and grace for you.

MILEPOST 64
WHEN JOY BECOMES OUR STRENGTH

Do not grieve, for the joy of the LORD is your strength (Nehemiah 8:10).

Joy is a treasure found in the dark places of life, in the shadows, in the storms, and in the dark of night. Joy is the gem we find when we're reaching for hope, and in finding hope, we discover joy.

Many things might make us *feel* happy, or we might *be* happy about a great many things. That's the point. Happiness is about *things* being exactly right. Situations. Circumstances. People. We base happiness on these. But joy is different. Joy likes to slip in the back door when it's least expected, when circumstances are not right, and when we seem to have no reason to find joy.

Joy is an oasis in the deserts of life. It's drawn from deep pools of hope and streams of faith. These streams and pools are replenished in only one way: by soaking in the presence of God, steeping ourselves in Him, and becoming more and more aware of how great His love is. We can allow dark times to drive us away from God, or we can purposefully draw nearer to God than ever before.

The context of Nehemiah 8:10 is a time of national repentance. People were mourning for their sinful ways, after which Nehemiah told them not to grieve any longer. That's not the same kind of grief as mourning the loss of a loved one. These words are not intended to say we shouldn't grieve for our loved one. However, the joy of the Lord being our strength is confirmed with enough other Scriptures that it is not misappropriating it to put it in context with our grief. Joy is also identified in Galatians 5:22 as a fruit of the Spirit. It is the joy *of the Lord*, the fruit of Him dwelling within us, not something we have to muster up on our own or deny our grief to obtain it.

Joy does not erase grief or minimize our loss. Rather, we find joy coexisting with grief. We discover a strength as strong as steel enabling us to endure with courage and grace. In joy, we discover optimism, resilience, and hope.

MILEPOST 65
SURFING MOTHER'S DAY

It's my third Mother's Day without Jeanette. This day will be emotional no matter what I do. Early in this grief journey, I learned grief comes in waves, and Mother's Day is a mighty big wave. The thought occurred to me. What if, instead of running from the waves, I surf them?

Whether we've ever gone surfing or not, haven't we all watched surfers? We see them paddle their boards out to where the waves are. They wait for the wave and for the exact moment to stand up and master it. We watch them glide smoothly, cutting through the water, confident and assured, and making the ride appear so easy. Of course, we know it's not easy.

Grief is like being on a surfboard in an emotional ocean. I'm out there in that ocean, watching the waves build. Here it comes—the huge wave known as Mother's Day. I can't ignore it, can't run away from it, and can't pretend it's not there. Instead, I must plant both feet firmly on the surfboard, steady myself as the wave comes, and allow it to carry me forward. I will master this wave, and I will not drown!

This analogy of surfing Mother's Day is simply my acknowledgment that I *can* get through this day, even though it's not easy. All the love and memories I have as a mother are worth celebrating, worth cherishing, and worth embracing. With so many blessings to be grateful for, this should not be a day I turn from or steel myself against. I should not seal off my heart from the feelings this day evokes. I will be a surfer, and I will conquer this wave.

Footsteps to Steady our Feet

Grief doesn't end, but it changes with the passing of time. How could I ever stop feeling the loss or stop missing Jeanette? I will always grieve for her because I can never stop loving her. But in due course, I am learning survival skills. I'm learning how to manage emotions as they come. I'm learning that the waves of grief will pass and that I can still be standing. I know I've said all these things before, but I need reminders. Repetition is necessary.

Are there some reminders you need to constantly repeat to yourself? Can you look back and see how far you've come? Journal about what has helped you. What reminders do you still need to hear? Can you see progress, even in little things? Take stock of where you are now and give yourself a round of applause and a pat on the back for the progress you've made. How can you reward yourself for making it this far?

Are there seasons, special days, or holidays you need surfing lessons to survive? How is the surfing analogy helpful in getting through difficult days without drowning in our sadness? Is there another analogy or comparison you can relate to better? What helps you get through days with strong emotional waves?

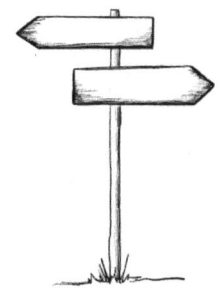

CHECKING THE MAP
DISCOVERING THE HEART OF AN ADVENTURER

MILESTONE 66
BROKEN BUT STILL SMILING

A decorative yellow smiley-face mug cheered Jeanette's students from its place on her desk when she was a teacher. After her Heaven-going, I brought the mug home and set it on a shelf in the room where I do most of my writing. I loved seeing the bright smiling face while I worked. That is, until I accidentally overloaded the shelf, and everything came crashing down. Books and other items scattered across the room. Nothing was broken *except* the smiling yellow mug. With a sad heart, I picked up the pieces, intending to throw them away. I set it on a filing cabinet while I continued cleaning up the rest of the fallen items. When I finished, I looked at that mug, still smiling, even with a broken handle and a piece broken out of it. Broken, but still smiling? What a perfect object lesson! Right then, I decided to keep the mug to remind me that it's possible to smile even after being broken. It is now glued back together—and still smiling.

Looking at that mug reminds me of this Scripture. "For God, who said, 'Let light shine out of darkness,' made his light shine in our hearts to give us the light of the knowledge of God's glory displayed in the face of Christ. But we have this treasure in jars of clay to show that this all-surpassing power is from God and not from us. We are hard pressed on every side, but not crushed; perplexed, but not in despair; persecuted, but not abandoned; struck down, but not destroyed" (2 Corinthians 4:6–9).

Many things can cause our lives to crash around us. I'm sure we've all picked up broken pieces and cleaned up messes in life. God is an expert at that. He can help. It's what He does. We may have been broken and glued back together, and we may have the scars to show for it, but we can still smile.

MILESTONE 67
RECALCULATING

Ever since my daughter's Heaven-going, I've been traveling unfamiliar roads in unknown territories. The landscape of my life is so altered from what it was. My internal GPS for the course of my life has been working overtime to steer me through this grief journey, adjusting and recalculating with each new day.

Unless they've navigated their own grief journey, few people understand it. That's one reason I write—to share what it's like to travel this road. A grief journey is so much more complex than maneuvering through emotional peaks and valleys. It's also a search for a new identity, a new sense of self, and a new purpose. It's a search for safety and security in a world that feels more precarious than before. It's a journey of discovery and of rebuilding, remaking, and reshaping a new life. It's a journey of trial and error, like trying to navigate through a maze.

Everyone has times of recalculating their lives, whether it's grief or some other kind of journey. Life is an adventure. Adventure can be challenging, stressful, and uninvited, but it also brings rewards. Recalculating life is not a comfortable process, but meandering paths often lead to beautiful destinations.

MILEPOST 68
WHAT'S NEXT, PAPA?

This resurrection life you received from God is not a timid, grave-tending life. It's adventurously expectant, greeting God with a childlike, "What's next, Papa?" (Romans 8:15 MSG).

In J. R. R. Tolkien's tale, *The Hobbit*, Bilbo reacts to Gandalf's invitation to an adventure by saying, "Nasty, disturbing, uncomfortable things! Make you late for dinner! I can't think what anybody sees in them."[14]

I should be a hobbit. I, too, prefer the comforts of home. I love my comfortable chair by the fire, great food, and a good book. Adventure? I can do without it, thank you. But to be honest, after all the time I've spent cocooned in my small sphere, I'm a bit antsy for some adventure. I'm still a homebody and an introvert, but a part of me longs to stretch my wings.

I feel the emptiness of Jeanette's absence, and I miss her so much, but one of the easiest ways to stay stuck in grief is to focus on that emptiness. I should not park, settle in, or become too comfortable in looking back and dwelling on the past. I must have expectations for the future, even if it's a different future than I expected. I must be forward-looking with the prospect of a new chapter in my life.

God calls me on to the next thing, the next adventure. Like Bilbo, I might hesitate, but after a while, the call of adventure is too much to resist. I do crave some adventure, after all. Just a little. Maybe a small one. No slaying of dragons. But I find myself asking Abba Father, "What's next, Papa?"

Are you ready for more adventures? It's okay if you're not there yet. It takes a while. We come to this milepost in our own time. Stay on the path and just keep putting one foot in front of the other. That's adventure enough.

MILEPOST 69
HEAVENLY PERSPECTIVE

Therefore, since we are surrounded by such a great cloud of witnesses, let us throw off everything that hinders and the sin that so easily entangles. And let us run with perseverance the race marked out for us, fixing our eyes on Jesus, the pioneer and perfecter of faith. For the joy set before him he endured the cross, scorning its shame, and sat down at the right hand of the throne of God .... Therefore, strengthen your feeble arms and weak knees. "Make level paths for your feet," so that the lame may not be disabled, but rather healed (Hebrews 12:1–2, 12–13).

Nothing brings healing to soul and spirit and all that ails me like being in nature. Camping provides a marvelous time of peace, meditation, and nurturing my spirit. It rejuvenates and refreshes me. One of the things I love is waking up early and going outside to witness the stars fade in the predawn sky.

While waiting for the sunrise, my mind drifts to questions I often wonder about, like how it is possible for joy and sadness to coexist. On one hand, I feel the sadness and void of missing Jeanette. On the other hand, I'm discovering new streams of joy and peace. How odd is that? I also wonder, as I have before, if it's okay for me to be happy without Jeanette. Why is that even a question? Of course, Jeanette wants me to find joy in life.

Our child in Heaven sees us recovering and beginning to live again. They rejoice to see our frail arms and weak legs becoming stronger and stronger. They love that we're finding new paths for our feet. It can hearten us to think of their perspective. Knowing that they're cheering for us enables us to journey on.

MILEPOST 70
WWJD?

Do you remember when the acronym WWJD was popular? The letters stood for "What Would Jesus Do?" It originated from a classic Christian book by Charles Sheldon called *In His Steps*. Not to be irreverent, but just because Jeanette's name fit the letters, we used to say "What Would Jeanette Do?"

WWJD has evolved into a new question: what would Jeanette want me to do with my life? How would she want me to live? We always think in terms of children carrying on their parents' legacy, but shouldn't it be an even stronger unction to carry on our child's legacy? What should we do with each passing day? It's a powerful incentive to think about what Jeanette would want me to do.

I am not Jeanette, and I can't be who she was. As I think about the concept of carrying on her legacy, I wonder exactly what that should look like. I don't have the same aptitude, skills, or the desire to do the same things she did. But what about those things I *can* do? What about things I enjoy doing that would qualify as carrying on her legacy? Jeanette knew how much I love to write and that one of my aspirations was to write a book someday. Yet during her lifetime, I never got around to it.

In fourth grade, I wrote my first short story—not as a school assignment, but just for fun—and from then on, I was hooked on writing. In high school, teachers commented on my writing ability, and I'm one of those nerdy people who actually enjoyed writing papers in college. But what became of my dream to be a published author? Perhaps I never had anything that I was truly passionate about or that lit a fire in me enough to write a book. Until now. What would Jeanette want me to do? I can almost hear her say, "Mom, get that book written!"

What is your story, dream, gift, or ability? What might your child be cheering for you to do? What might be a goal for you to pursue? I encourage you to explore the possibilities.

Footsteps for Adventurers

Forget the former things; do not dwell on the past. See, I am doing a new thing! Now it springs up; do you not perceive it? I am making a way in the wilderness and streams in the wasteland (Isaiah 43:18–19).

Life can still be a yo-yo of good and bad days, but I love moments when I can set grieving aside and truly feel alive again. I'm thankful for respites, such as going camping and being out in nature. I'm surprised when a sense of contentment and lightness of heart settles over me and when I feel the soul-soothing assurance that life is still worth living. I didn't know if I could ever feel like that again. God truly is doing new things, blazing a trail through the wilderness, and surprising me with streams in the desert places of life. It makes me *want* to keep going. What will God surprise me with next? What's around the next bend? I have to keep going to find out.

But for all of that, it's still so easy to slip into negativity about the future. Worry, anxiety, and pessimism are apt to be our default setting. We automatically go there because of what we've experienced. But we can't allow what happened to be the primary programmer of our minds. We have to intentionally take charge of our thoughts and reprogram our default setting to positive thoughts, gratitude, and a sense of adventure in life.

Here are some helpful Scriptures and a few questions for journaling about forming new thought habits:

"Be transformed by the renewing of your mind," (Romans 12:2). How can renewing our minds be a healing factor in transforming our grief? In what specific areas does your mind need to be renewed to further your healing process?

"We take captive every thought to make it obedient to Christ," (2 Corinthians 10:5b). What does it mean to take every thought captive? How can this be part of our healing process?

Do not be anxious or worried about anything, but in everything [every circumstance and situation] by prayer and petition with thanksgiving, continue to make your [specific] requests known to God. And the peace of God [that peace which reassures the heart, that peace] which transcends all understanding, [that peace which] stands guard over your hearts and your minds in Christ Jesus [is yours]. Finally, believers, whatever is true, whatever is honorable and worthy of respect, whatever is right and confirmed by God's word, whatever is pure and wholesome, whatever is lovely and brings peace, whatever is admirable and of good repute; if there is any excellence, if there is anything worthy of praise, think continually on these things [center your mind on them, and implant them in your heart] (Philippians 4:6–8 AMP).

I love the expansion that the Amplified Version brings to Scriptures. It can be a worthwhile exercise to write out Scriptures, expanding them so that they speak to us personally. In your journal, expand verses you read as they apply to you. Include specific ways to improve your thoughts, renew your mind, and create new thought habits.

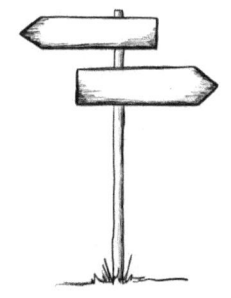

SHADOWY PATHWAYS
FINDING THE LIGHT

MILEPOST 71
CANYONS

For our first Thanksgiving without Jeanette, we splurged on an amazing trip to the Grand Canyon via the Grand Canyon Railroad. That trip is still a wonderful memory. Two years later, the Canyon again beckoned us to spend Thanksgiving there. But not by train this time. Instead, we returned as campers.

I could spend hours admiring the spectacular vistas and reveling in the Grand Canyon's splendor. The sight never gets old, no matter how many times we visit. Perhaps I love it now more than ever for what it represents to me. The Grand Canyon would not exist if it had not been carved by devastating and destructive forces: volcanoes, floods, erosion, disaster, upheaval, and catastrophe. All of that so that we could hike trails, raft waters, and stand on bluffs, peering across the vast expanse, too amazed for words.

I ponder the canyon that exists in my heart: the void, the emptiness, the vast chasm in my life without Jeanette.

Yet emerging from the devastation and cataclysm of her loss, I find grace, beauty, and tempered strength that wasn't there before. I return to this Scripture from Isaiah 61 as I consider God's purpose to transform the destruction in my life. How is God taking the rubble of your life and rebuilding something new?

"God sent me to announce the year of his grace ... to comfort all who mourn, To care for the needs of all who mourn in Zion, give them bouquets of roses instead of ashes, Messages of joy instead of news of doom, a praising heart instead of a languid spirit. Rename them "Oaks of Righteousness" planted by God to display his glory. They'll rebuild the old ruins, raise a new city out of the wreckage. They'll start over on the ruined cities, take the rubble left behind and make it new. Instead of your shame you will receive a double portion, and instead of disgrace you will rejoice in your inheritance. And so you will inherit a double portion in your land, and everlasting joy will be yours" (Isaiah 61:1–4, 7 MSG).

MILEPOST 72
WHAT TO DO WITH CHRISTMAS WHEN THE WHOLE WORLD IS AWRY

The pinnacle of our year has always been Christmas. Filled with all thing joyful—laughter and love; surprises and wonder; twinkling lights and candles; nativity scenes and Jesus's birth; movies and musicals; cookies and treats; decorations and gift wrapping; snowflakes and Santa—the whole shebang!

But it's different now. Christmas feels odd, awry, askew, like a picture on the wall that hangs crooked and can't be straightened no matter what I do. Because it's not the picture. The wall is all out of kilter—the wall, the house, the whole world—everything. Which is why the picture can't be straightened.

It's peculiar to realize Christmas (indeed, the whole month of December) will never be the same again. I cling to our happy traditions even though they feel hollow now. I fight to accept that life has changed, and it's all right to change traditions and adapt. But that's the point. I resent having to change long-standing traditions. I feel guilty leaving out activities that we used to do. Letting go feels wrong.

I fight for normalcy. I fight to straighten the picture of what Christmas is supposed to look like. It's a losing battle, though. The picture, the walls, the house, the world—they're all askew. "I will enjoy Christmas!" I shout defiantly—but give me a moment to grieve the loss of Christmases past. Although some people give up celebrating holidays after the death of a loved one, I will not relinquish my Christmas. I'll find a way to enjoy it. If I can't straighten the picture, I'll frame it in twinkly lights. *I will not give up on Christmas.*

Sometimes it's easier to let go of celebrations and holidays because they're difficult, but that's not the answer. It *is* a battle to figure out what to do, but it's a battle worth fighting.

MILEPOST 73
TUNNELS

Grief journeys take many twists and turns: uphill, downhill, and every which way. There are days when I'm fine, when skies are sunny, and it's almost as if nothing has changed. But around the next bend, the sun disappears, and suddenly I'm in a dark gray funk again.

Something always triggers those dark days, even something as small as the waft of a scent or the snatch of a song. Sometimes a random thought runs through my mind and triggers the darkness. I didn't see the ambush coming, but an involuntary grayness settles over me. It feels like passing through a tunnel. One moment, there's light, and the next it's dark.

Some tunnels are longer than others, and some are darker or colder. But a tunnel is not a dead end. Our footsteps will always lead us back to sunlight if we keep on walking. Recognize the tunnel for what it is: not a dead end but a path to the other side of the mountain. It does lead back to the light. Just. Keep. Going.

"For though I fall, I will rise again. Though I sit in darkness, the Lord will be my light" (Micah 7:8 NLT).

MILESTONE 74
ANOTHER BIRTHDAY IN HEAVEN

Oh yes, you shaped me first inside, then out; you formed me in my mother's womb. I thank you, High God—you're breathtaking! Body and soul, I am marvelously made! I worship in adoration—what a creation! You know me inside and out, you know every bone in my body; You know exactly how I was made, bit by bit, how I was sculpted from nothing into something. Like an open book, you watched me grow from conception to birth; all the stages of my life were spread out before you, the days of my life all prepared before I'd even lived one day. Your thoughts—how rare, how beautiful! God, I'll never comprehend them! I couldn't even begin to count them—any more than I could count the sand of the sea. Oh, let me rise in the morning and live always with you (Psalm 139:13–18 MSG).

How impossible it would be to forget the day of my daughter's birth—the day she came into the world and we glimpsed her sweet, precious face for the first time.

I am so blessed to have been Jeanette's mother! How empty and barren our lives would have been without her presence. Though absent now, the blessing of her life remains.

I will always celebrate her birthday because I'm so grateful for her life. But as her birthday approaches, I miss her more than ever. Each passing year, I want to do something special in her honor, but I feel so drained of strength. It's hard to plan something and even harder to implement it.

The way you choose to honor the birthday of a loved one in Heaven is personal. People do many different things. I think celebrating her birthday should be specific to her personality, her memory, and our relationship. Thinking about all this and putting a plan into action can exhaust me when I'm already emotionally depleted. So it's important to remind myself that whatever I choose to do on her birthday is not a measure of my love for her. If I only have energy to do something small, it indicates the limits of my strength, not my love.

This year, I bought some small bottles of bubble solution and a group of us went outside and blew bubbles. It was great fun! We laughed so much, and I think Jeanette was laughing along with us. I'm sure she loved it.

Our child's birthday is precious even though it breaks our hearts, and we miss them so dearly. They lived, and they were a treasure. Even the babies we never met who never had a true birthday are worthy of our remembrance. They will never be forgotten as long as we live.

MILEPOST 75
ANOTHER ANNIVERSARY OF THAT DAY

I felt barely alive the first year. The second year, I continued to exist in my cocoon, coming out of hibernation occasionally and then retreating. Approaching the third anniversary of Jeanette's Heaven-going, I feel as if winter is slowly receding and melting into a pale spring. Life is very different now. Many chapters in my life came to an end the day Jeanette died, but new chapters are being written. Here are a few things I've learned.

Nurturing close relationships is a greater priority than ever. It's not about the quantity of relationship but about their quality. I'd rather invest in a few deep friendships than have many superficial relationships.

I'm not into people-pleasing nearly as much as I used to be. I'm more comfortable with myself and who I am. I don't have to offer an explanation or apologize for my choices. People can accept me or not, and I don't need to make them happy.

The emotional stress following the death of a child (even an adult child) can make or break a marriage. The trauma will likely expose cracks that already existed in the relationship that will either widen or be forged together by the fire. I am blessed by the forging of our marriage so that it's now stronger than ever.

Grief will test a person's mettle to the core and make a person bitter or better. Which one we become is not about how strong or brave we are but about the everyday choices we make to adjust our attitudes, forgive, let go of what we can't change, and to be willing to change what we can.

I miss Jeanette, and I always will. I weave in and out of sadness, sometimes ambushed by emotions that hit me like a wrecking ball. Even so, it's not the raw, ragged, open wound nor the deep, dark pit that it was at first. It's true: grief never ends, and I still ache. I've learned grief exists because love exists, and I will always love and miss my dear Jeanette.

It is an honor to share my journey with other bereaved parents. As fellow travelers on the road, our experiences and stories may widely differ. Yet something bonds grievers together and bereaved parents even tighter than most. We identify and empathize with one another in a way that no one who hasn't experienced this type of loss can. We find an indescribable preciousness in the ability to embrace and comfort other parents who have lost a child because we know what it's like. I've discovered this incredible truth: as difficult as it is to believe at first, surviving is possible, and so is learning to thrive.

Footsteps Toward the Light

Working through conflicting feelings and doubts about God is an important part of our healing. Being angry with God may be a natural response in our brokenness while we work through the many questions we're likely to face. However, dwelling in that anger will not bring peace. It will stall and hinder our recovery and ability to find hope. God isn't the cause of bad things that happen, but He is the one who can transform them into good. God turns tragedy to triumph so that we can rise from the ashes and live again.

God proves His absolute goodness and fathomless love by walking every step of this journey alongside us. He weeps with us and uplifts our heavy hearts when we're so laden with grief, we wonder how we'll ever go on. It's impossible to overstate or exaggerate the depths of His love for us. But our awareness and sense of God's love and presence may be hindered by our emotions. Sadness, depression, fear, and anger, for example, can be so intense, it's hard to feel anything else. It doesn't mean God isn't with us or doesn't care about us.

We know we're supposed to rely on faith rather than feelings, but that can be super challenging when grieving. Yet it is so vital. Something happens when we honestly admit, "God, I can barely believe in You right now, and Your love seems lost. I feel abandoned. I don't know where You are, but I chose to believe You're with me, even if I can't feel You anywhere in this mess." If we persist in expressing faith, regardless of how we feel, a breakthrough *will* come.

Likewise, I cannot overstate the necessity of looking for value in each day. Focusing on the positive and nurturing an optimistic outlook is essential, especially on the dark days. We need to keep pressing on in faith until we find light again. It's just around the corner, and we'll find it if we *don't give up.*

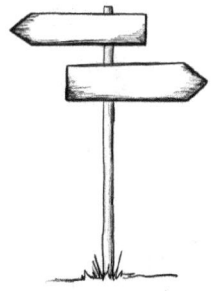

ROCKY ROADS
THE IMPORTANCE OF RESILIENCE

MILEPOST 76
LIFE IS A BOUNCY HOUSE

I see metaphors everywhere. Combine my propensity for finding metaphors with my sense of humor, and who knows what I'll come up with. A friend posted about a bouncy house on Facebook, and my mind ran with it, so this is my metaphor of a bouncy house.

Life is like a bouncy house, full of ups and downs. We fall. We rise. No matter how many ups and downs we experience, the important thing is to keep getting up. We fall. We rise. And therein lies the whole point. It's about resilience. Bouncing back. The ability to get up and go on.

This metaphor might seem simplistic and even a bit silly, but, it's true, isn't it? One of our most important life skills is the ability to get back up when life knocks us down. Because life will do that, whether it's the death of a loved one or any number of other losses, traumas, tragedies, or hardships. No matter what happens, we need to know how to bounce back.

So how do we bounce back? Is resilience a natural skill? No! It's an acquired skill, a combination of three essentials: faith in God, friends who aid us, and our own cooperation and willingness. That last one is key. Without our own willingness and cooperation to get back on our feet, no one else will be able to help us much. And yet, all three components—God, others, and our own cooperation—are necessary. We need to learn how to be as resilient as kids playing in a bouncy house. Fall and get back up. Accept the hand of a friend helping us up and help each other up.

"The Lord upholds all who fall and lifts up all who are bowed down" (Psalm 145:14).

"Though the righteous fall seven times, they rise again" (Proverbs 24:16).

"Though one may be overpowered, two can defend themselves. A cord of three strands is not quickly broken" (Ecclesiastes 4:12).

MILEPOST 77
UNSHAKABLE

Therefore everyone who hears these words of mine and puts them into practice is like a wise man who built his house on the rock. The rain came down, the streams rose, and the winds blew and beat against that house; yet it did not fall, because it had its foundation on the rock (Matthew 7:24–25).

I'm not going to tell you that child loss won't shake your whole world. It will. After writing that statement, I must stop, put my pen down, and pause a moment. I try not to let my thoughts return to the day Jeanette died, or the day after, and relive the awful terribleness of it. When I allow the memory to return, it is as fresh as the day it happened, so I must pause a moment before continuing.

More than any other experience, child loss has shaken me to the core. But as the days, weeks, and months began to pass, something astonishing happened. *I was still standing!* How was that even possible? It seemed inconceivable. And yet, day by day, I somehow kept on going. No one could be more surprised than me that I was surviving.

The potential misunderstanding is how strong I must be. People think that I must be an amazing person to still be standing after my loss. No, that is not it. Being unshakable is not because *I* am strong but because of *who* and *what* I'm trusting and believing in. Because *God* is unshakable, I am unshakable.

I may be perplexed by life. I may be thrown into a dungeon of darkness by events. I may *feel* very shaken indeed, and yet I am unshakable. My faith holds firm, no matter what kind of shaking is going on. During a recent sermon at church, I jotted this note: "We don't downsize God in the face of our giants. We downsize our giants in the face of God."[15] In other words, we become unshakable when we rely on God and on His unchangeable, unshakable nature. No matter what changes life brings, God remains the same (Malachi 3:6, Hebrews 13:8). When we exchange our thoughts and attitudes for the mind of Christ (1 Corinthians 2:16), we discover the overcoming life of the kingdom. When we become unshakable in Christ, we cannot be made weaker or destroyed, no matter how much we're shaken.

Through the rain of tears, through the storms of turbulent emotions, and through the dark days, we can remain unshakable if we stand firm in our belief that God is good, that life can still be good, and that we have a purpose for living. Those beliefs make us unshakable.

MILEPOST 78
BEREAVED MOTHER'S DAY

Did you know the first Sunday in May is set aside for honoring bereaved mothers? It's called International Bereaved Mother's Day, established in 2010. How many women do you know who have experienced a miscarriage; stillbirth; infant loss; child or teen loss; or adult child loss? You might think you don't know anyone, but perhaps you know more of these women than you realize.

Few people talk about the *m* word: miscarriage. According to the Mayo Clinic, at least 10 to 20 percent of pregnancies end in a miscarriage.[16] Miscarriages can be terribly devastating, yet so often, women are pushed to accept the loss and move on as if it was nothing.

For decades, I never told anyone that I had a miscarriage. I buried the memory and lost track of it until a series of recent events reminded me of it. As the months and years passed, I convinced myself I must have been mistaken. It was so early in my pregnancy, maybe I wasn't really pregnant. At least, that's the lie I told myself until I believed it. Since it was so long ago, it might seem like it doesn't matter anymore, but it most certainly does. Now I realize how important it is to remember and come to terms with what happened. By denying my miscarriage, I was also denying my child's existence—a child who was so dearly wanted and a child who was Jeanette's younger brother or sister. Yes, he or she matters! Even after all the years of denial, I feel a connection with this child of mine that I've never met, and I've had to process through belated grief over the loss.

As women, we should be able to talk to each other and comfort each other about these sensitive topics. We shouldn't hide our scars. We should share our experiences and how we've survived and how they changed us. The purpose of Bereaved Mother's Day is not only to honor mothers with a child in Heaven but also to raise awareness of this subject. Child loss shouldn't be a taboo subject.

When a child dies, yes, it is awkward to know what to say, but even if words fall short, you can show you care. You don't need to have all the answers. No one does. Don't try to take away the pain. No one can. But anyone can listen without judgment. Allow a bereaved mother to talk about her child and her experience, but don't pry or ask for more details than she is comfortable sharing. Allow her to be real. Allow her time to figure out her life and who she is after her loss. Be a friend. Be kind. And *please,* don't expect her to just "get over it." If you are a bereaved mother, when you feel up to it, don't be afraid to share your story. You don't know what a comfort you might be to someone else.

Every loss is unique and individual. That is exactly why we need each other. We need to share our stories. Bereaved Mother's Day is important so that we can share our journeys, help each other heal, and raise awareness of what it's like to walk this path.

MILEPOST 79
WHAT I WANT FOR MOTHER'S DAY

What if my daughter is forgotten? What if I don't hear Jeanette's name spoken anymore? What if no one remembers I was Jeanette's mom? What if that entire portion of my life fades into the shadows of the past until no one even knows it happened?

The importance of remembering grows greater with each passing year. The sands of time begin to bury her life on earth a little bit deeper year by year. Even now, I meet people who never knew her, and I struggle to describe her to them in a meaningful way. No matter how many photographs I show and for all my talk of Jeanette-this and Jeanette-that, she remains one-dimensional to those who never met her. How I wish you could have known her!

I loved being a mother. Being Jeanette's mom was the best blessing of my life and gave me purpose, identity, and a reason to live for so many wonderful years. I not only want Jeanette to be remembered, I want to be remembered and acknowledged as her mother. My role is worth celebrating. Being Jeanette's mom deserves *some* recognition. And yet I feel so much ambivalence about Mother's Day, and it's hard to know what to do with it.

Mother's Day is among the most difficult days for a mother whose child is in Heaven. All the same, don't be afraid to speak the child's name. Tell about a memory you have and let us share our memories. You aren't reminding us that our child died; you're remembering that they lived and that we were their mother. And oh, what a precious gift that is.

MILEPOST 80
NO ONE TO CALL ME GRANDMA

Have you noticed that within each loss, there are multiple losses? One of our losses, since Jeanette was our only child, is not having grandchildren. I am only beginning to come to terms with what it means not to be "Grandma." I've pushed this loss to a back burner because of more immediate losses, but this one is now coming more and more to the forefront.

Secondary losses are things we don't get to experience as the result of losing our child. Depending on the age of a child, it might mean never taking them to the first day of kindergarten, never taking pictures on prom night, never being mother of the bride or groom, or in my case, never holding a newborn grandchild in my arms. We must unpack and grieve the loss of each of these missed experiences as we reach them. This is one more thing no one ever told me about grief. We will have to unwrap multiple layers of loss as the years go by.

In my journey, I've learned the only way through grief is to grieve. Whatever the loss is, we must face it, own it, acknowledge it, and walk through it. Cry it out and be sad, but work through it. Getting through grief does not mean coming to the end of it, though. Secondary losses will arise as time goes by. Our hearts will break afresh. But as we come to each new milepost and each new loss, God has special grace awaiting, and He will walk us through it step by step.

Psalm 131:2 talks about "cultivating a quiet heart like a baby content in its mother's arms" (MSG). In my mind, I picture a baby who's been crying and is now being held closely and lovingly until they fall asleep comforted. That is a picture of us in our Heavenly Father's arms. That's the place we need to find in grieving each of our losses—loved, comforted, and held close.

On the practical side of not having grandchildren is the possibility of filling that role with other children. Frankly, I'm not ready for that yet, but maybe at some point in the future I will be. I know opportunities exist in the church and community with children who need a grandparent figure in their lives. It's not the same as having our own grandchildren, but it could fill a need in a child's life and mine.

Not being a grandparent is another enormous loss for parents of an only child. But we will get through this loss as we get through all our other losses—allowing ourselves to grieve the loss, seeking God, finding our peace in Him, and last, but not least, healing our broken hearts by reaching out to someone who needs our love.

Footsteps for Overcoming

Much of our healing comes from taking time to be still and soak in the presence of God, listening to worship music, meditating on God's Word, and believing the Holy Spirit is ministering to the deep places of our soul. In this kind of intimacy with God, we find a reawakening of our trust and renewal in our relationship with Him. Coming to Him even with our doubts, questions, and conflicts, gives Him a chance to heal broken places in our relationship.

People might commonly struggle to get their bearings again in their relationship with God after the death of their child. We might then think we've driven Him away through our doubts or negativity. Please don't think that. Hebrews 4:16 assures us that we can "approach God's throne of grace with confidence, so that we may receive mercy and find grace to help us in our time of need." We come to a throne of grace, not a throne of judgment. No matter what condition our hearts are in, we'll find mercy, grace, and strength, not retribution or rebuke. Our best source of strength, comfort, and healing is in God's presence. We have a standing invitation to come to Him with full assurance that we are always welcomed, accepted, and loved.

So much encouragement that God speaks to us is lost because we didn't write it down. Be sure to keep journaling and recording every little blessing and victory and put it in your treasure chest to remind yourself of it later. We do need those reminders.

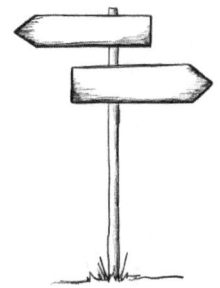

POUNDING THE PAVEMENT
SOLDIERING ON MILE AFTER MILE

MILEPOST 81
WASH, RINSE, REPEAT

I should know by now that there's no escaping grief. As much as I may try to run away from it, it's still here. Even when I shove it aside and try to avoid it, it is ever present. I'm tired of grieving. I'm tired of tears. I'm tired of the emotional roller coaster. I find brief respites when I'm busy and distracted, but grief always returns.

I already know that losing Jeanette is a wound as real as any physical wound. I already know that grief takes a toll on physical health. But I didn't know it would *still* be like this four years later. I don't want to grieve anymore. I want to be over and done with it. So once again, I made the mistake of trying to wall it off and pretend I'm fine. Not pretending for other people, but trying to convince myself I'm fine.

I discovered I can no more stop the flow of grief than turn off the waters of Niagara Falls like a faucet. As years go by, a kind of normalcy has returned. My daily routines have become reestablished. It's easy to conveniently "forget" about grief. Ah, but therein lies the problem. I *am* still grieving! I can't turn off the grief faucet just because I'm tired of it.

My on-going struggle does not mean it never gets better. There is a vast difference between my grief now and the early days of grieving. I've experienced so much healing, and it's not nearly as dark as it was in the beginning. But I still weave in and out of good days and not-so-good days. I still have days when I need to stop and give myself permission to rest. Even after four years, I still need more recovery. I jotted the following lines in my journal, because I need this reminder to go easy on myself even now.

> Remember to be gentle,
> Remember to be kind,
> Remember to be patient,
> It's an uphill climb.

MILEPOST 82
THE WILL TO LIVE

Grief made me a hypochondriac. I worry about my health and my husband's health all the time. It's not so strange, considering our daughter died suddenly from ailments we didn't even know she had. But here's the odd thing. I fret about our health, and yet I haven't done anything about it.

A recent cancer scare raised some uncomfortable questions about how I regard my health. Specifically, I wondered if I would accept treatment if the tests returned positive. My thoughts leaned strongly toward declining chemo if the need should arise. Thankfully, the tests were negative. I do not have cancer. But the attitudes stirred up by this close call deserved serious examination. Shouldn't I do everything I can to live? Shouldn't I at least *want* to do everything I can? But why prolong this life when a better one is waiting?

The fallacy in my thinking was exposed as more health issues arose. Neglect had taken its toll on my body. My weight, always a problem, had reached an all-time high, and my body was crying out for help with numerous signals and symptoms. Change came with a growing fear of not living long enough to publish my book. (I told you I was a hypochondriac.) I'm sure my fear was an exaggeration, but it produced the turning point leading me to action.

I'm including this experience as a cautionary tale. Some consequences of grief can be quite subtle. Not taking care of ourselves falls in that category. It's easy for a lackadaisical attitude toward life and health to creep in almost undetected. Thoughts of a joyful reunion with my daughter in Heaven are one thing, but foolishly rushing toward the pearly gates is something entirely different. That doesn't mean I'm suicidal, but an I-don't-care attitude is definitely detrimental to health.

The will to live has a great deal to do with our sense of purpose. For parents who lost their only child, it's so crucial for us to find our purpose because we have no generations following us to live for. But if we're still here on this earth, we still have tasks to complete.

Jeremiah 29:11 promises God has a purpose, a future, and hope for us. Not only that, but we were created with a purpose. Ephesians 2:10 says, "He creates each of us by Christ Jesus to join him in the work he does, the good work he has gotten ready for us to do, work we had better be doing" (MSG).

James 1:5 tells us that God will give us wisdom when we ask, and Proverbs 3:5–6 promises direction when we need it. Believe me, no one needs wisdom, direction, a sense of purpose, and hope for the future more than a grieving parent. We can find all these things in God as we seek Him and allow Him to lead us.

Living to be one hundred is not my goal but living to complete the purpose for which I'm here certainly is. My will to live is stronger now, and I'm taking care of myself with more gratitude for each day I'm alive.

MILESTONE 83
FESTIVUS — THE GRIEVER'S EDITION

In a 1997 *Seinfeld* episode, George's father, Frank Costanza, made up an anti-consumer holiday he called "Festivus." Instead of a Christmas tree, there was an unadorned aluminum pole, and instead of remembering the blessings of the year, complaints and grievances were aired. He called it "Festivus for the rest of us."[17]

Maybe we grievers should make up our own version of Festivus. Dispense with the glittery, holly-jolly falderal. Who needs all that sugary sweetness of the season when our hearts are broken and tears drown out every happy note? Let's make up our own celebration. We'll call it Festivus—The Griever's Edition.

Of course, I'm being as facetious as that Seinfeld episode. But I am honestly acknowledging that holidays are not merry and bright for everyone. Rather the holiday season can be a cold, dark, weary time for grievers. We carry memories of happier times that will not and cannot ever be repeated because of a vacancy no one can fill. An empty chair at the table. A stocking not hung anymore. The hollowness inside us that's numb to holiday cheer. And worse yet, so few people understand what we're going through. No one really gets it except other grievers. That's why I suggest a Festivus for grievers.

No doubt about it. It's a rough time of year. But do I really want to chuck it all, dust off my hands, and walk away from the holiday season, bitter? Is nothing salvageable in the wreck and ruin of my traditions? I sift through the remnants of our holidays past like one searching through the debris after a fire or flood. I fall to my knees in tears over the loss, the devastation, and all that will never be recovered. But then, I lift my eyes to the heavens and declare, "We are hard pressed on every side, but not crushed; perplexed, but not in despair … struck down, but not destroyed" (2 Corinthians 4:8–9).

Something still remains about Christmas that refuses to cave in to the cynicism of Festivus. Hope. Peace. Love. Joy. These virtues of Advent weave their way into my brokenness. Hope for the future and belief that life, though not the same, can still be blessed. Peace in knowing that no matter what happens, God is with us. Love that reaches beyond self to see and care for the needs of others. Yes, even joy, because joy is more than superficial happiness. It transcends circumstances and our grief. Joy is a deep place in the heart where rivers of hope, peace, and love converge into an ocean—an ocean that flows from one humble origin—a Babe in a manger. Without that Baby, we might as well dispense with the pretense and have our Festivus. Indeed, the holiday season and all its trapping is empty and void of purpose without that glorious birth. Forget Festivus! Thank God, there is more to Christmas than paper and tinsel.

It is all too easy to let bitterness, cynicism, sadness, hollowness, or numbness swallow up the happy and beautiful things about the Christmas season. This is our fifth Christmas without Jeanette. Even though I know the Christmas story by heart, I'm rereading it from Matthew and Luke along with the prophecies about the coming Messiah as if I've never read them before (e.g., Isaiah 7:14, Isaiah 9:6, and Isaiah 53–54). They ease my soul and bring fresh peace to my troubled heart as I refocus on the Baby, the story of His coming, and why He came.

MILEPOST 84
LET THE WEAK SAY, "I AM STRONG"

I don't know if this surreal feeling will ever go away. I still shake my head and wonder how it could be that she's not here. As I approach the milepost of another anniversary of Jeanette's Heaven-going, I realize I probably won't ever get used to this. Get through it, yes. But get used to it? No. Life is so different now. I still struggle to adapt. This time of year, after trudging through the holidays and passing the milepost of her birthday, I arrive at the five-year anniversary of her Heaven-going, emotionally and spiritually spent. I'm worn down and worn out. Tired. Weary. Broken.

That's how I feel, but I remind myself that I am not my feelings. That is not who I am. Today in my journaling, I felt compelled to write down who I really am despite how I feel. My identity comes from God and His Word, not my feelings or circumstances. Some days, it's not enough just to write the words in my journal,

I need to say them out loud. I don't feel like it, but I know I need to in order to get it deep down in my heart.

Patients in the hospital recovering from surgery don't feel like getting out of bed, but the nurses make them do it anyway. In the same way, speaking these declarations out loud is for my healing, regardless of whether I *feel* like it. Plus it builds my faith to hear my own voice declaring these truths over myself.

These affirmations of faith help me stand on what God says about me rather than what my feelings say. I wrote them down as they came to my mind and not in any particular order. Here goes. Time to declare them out loud:

Let the weak say, "I am strong."
Let the broken say, "I am whole."
Let the griever say, "I can rejoice."
Let the wounded say, "I am healed."
Let the dead soul say, "I am alive in God."
Let the weary say, "I am revived."
Let the one who has hit rock bottom say, "I am rising."
Let the mourner say, "I am comforted."
Let the overwhelmed say, "I am an overcomer."
Let the victim say, "I have victory."
Let the prisoner say, "I am free."
Let the helpless say, "God is my helper."
Let the confused and perplexed say, "I understand what to do."
Let the defeated say, "I can do all things through Christ who gives me strength."

What are some affirmations for yourself that you could add in your journal? Write them down and remember to speak them as well as write them.

MILEPOST 85
SECRETS TO SURVIVAL

The day that altered my life forever came unexpected, unforeseen, and without warning. When my daughter, my only child died, people wondered how I'd survive. I wondered too. I would not have believed that survival was possible. And yet, somehow, from somewhere inside me, a strength arose I had no idea I even possessed. Where did it come from—this ability to rise from the ashes like a phoenix? What's my secret? How can a mother not only survive but thrive after such an unimaginable loss? Four keys are crucial for survival.

Expect Blessings

In spite of what happened, I expect blessings from God. I lean into Romans 8:28 until it's absorbed into my soul like healing ointment absorbed into a wound. I expect God to turn tragedy into triumph no matter how horrible I feel, no matter how bleak everything appears. I expect blessings from the goodness of God's heart.

Hold on to Hope

Some days, it seems as though all that's left to hang on to is barely a smidgen of hope. Yet I cling to it like a drowning person clings to a life raft. I clench my hands around hope like a climber hanging by a thread on the side of a mountain. I hope for better days ahead. I hope for a future that's not as dismal as my fears project. Jeremiah 29:11 promises that my future is in God's hands. I mix faith with my spoken words and project hope, not fear, into the future.

Trust

I choose to be confident in the goodness and faithfulness of God. What happened was not God's fault. It wasn't because God failed. If I want to blame someone or something, I turn my anger on the devil. He is the one who comes to steal, kill, and destroy. But God is the One who comforts me, strengthens me, and helps me—daily, hourly, and minute by minute. He keeps me putting one foot in front of the other. He is faithful and trustworthy to be my light in the darkness, my peace in the storm, and my comfort in sorrow.

Be Thankful

I am thankful for how God has proven Himself faithful amid this great loss. I'm thankful for all the daily miracles of His grace and blessings. I'm thankful for His tenderness and compassion, for giving me songs in the night, for the tears He sheds side by side with me, and for glimpses of the substantial reality of Heaven and its glory. As I begin to give thanks, my eyes are opened to see that His blessings are more numerous than the sands on the seashore. But if I'm not cultivating a thankful heart, I will walk blindly past His blessings without even being aware of them.

The ability to rise from the ashes of devastating loss is not innately in me. I didn't pull strength or hope out of a hat. I seriously would not have survived apart from God's grace and through cooperating with God in these four significant ways: expecting blessings, holding on to hope, trusting, and being thankful. Otherwise, I absolutely would crumble under the weight of sorrow. But God is greater than tragedy, greater than loss, greater than sorrow. His greatness lives within me and causes me to triumph. Life can be tragic and terrible, but God is by our side to give us strength.

"But the LORD stood at my side and gave me strength" (2 Timothy 4:17).

Footsteps for Weary Travelers

Do you know why military troops call cadence when they're marching? Not only does it serve to keep everyone in step, it also gives soldiers something else to focus their attention on during long marches. Every muscle of their body may be screaming, and they may feel near collapse from weariness. Cadence helps take their mind off their pain and fatigue, so they can push past it and keep going.

We grievers need something like cadence to help take our minds off our grief fatigue. We may know the importance and the benefits of renewing our minds and thinking higher, better thoughts, but it often requires more than that. We need to talk to ourselves and hear our own voices speaking positive, encouraging, uplifting declarations. We need to become our own best cheerleaders and raise a rousing cheer for ourselves out loud.

The affirmations I wrote in Milepost 84 and other similar declarations have made a world of difference in my life. Speaking out affirmations and declarations can powerfully replace negative thinking with positive thoughts. It also helps us be a "doer of the word, and not a hearer only" (James 1:22).

Writing out Bible verses and personalizing them with first person pronouns (I, me, my, mine) is a great way to begin making declarations. You can fill pages in your journal by finding the verses that apply best to you and your circumstances. Books are also available with Scripture affirmations and declarations.

CROSSROADS
CHOICES MATTER

MILEPOST 86
ASKING WHY

From the broken, ravaged depths of the darkest darkness we've ever known, we cry out, "Why?" The wrongness, senselessness, and injustice of our child's death demands an answer! But instead of answers, the Heavens seem silent, a silence that feels as wrong as the death itself.

No matter how versed in biblical answers we may be, they can feel so hollow when standing at the graveside of our child. No answer seems suitable. No answer justifies this loss. Sometimes, I think if God Himself came down and explained why this happened, we would argue with Him. We just want our child back.

God is big enough to handle the rawness of our emotions. We can take it all to Him. Dump it on Him. Pour everything out to Him. He has an incredible way of restoring peace to our soul in the midst of the storm, even if we don't get the answers we want. But a word of caution. Like milk that sits out too long, anger and bitterness left too long will turn sour. Going to God, even if—*especially* if—we're hurt and angry will keep it from turning rancid in our soul.

I hear about miracles of healing, even of people being raised from the dead, and it's a legitimate question, "Why not my child? Why wasn't my child healed?" I don't know. But here's what I do know. Sometimes the greater miracle is displayed in how we go on living afterward. The fact that we can get up each morning and go on living without our child is a *miracle*. It's a straight-up *miracle* because it is so tremendously hard, and yet we somehow manage to do it.

Asking the right questions is a major key to moving forward. How do we go on living? What do we do now? Where does this path lead? These are better questions to ask than "why." Of course, we want to know why. It's not wrong to ask. But to continue holding on to that question is the same as holding on to anger. It will eventually turn sour and rancid. Before that happens, we must begin to ask different questions—questions that do have answers.

Not why, but how? How do we get past this? Not why, but what? What do we do now? Not why, but where? Where is the light in this darkness? Instead of beating against the brick wall of why, we need to turn and find a new direction. No matter how dark it seems, we must stand on the precipice of each new day, expectantly looking for light and hope to return.

Not a day goes by that I don't miss Jeanette, some days more intensely than others. When it comes to child loss, there is no end to grief because I must live without my daughter for the rest of my life. It defies the natural order of things. It's not supposed to be that way, and it feels so wrong. With or without Jeanette, however, God is still good.

John 10:10 points to the "thief" (our spiritual enemy) as the one who steals, kills, and destroys. But God? *God* is the one who brings and restores abundant life. In restoring life to us, He paints each day with love and faithfulness. He comforts our broken hearts. He bathes us in peace beyond comprehension (Philippians 4:7).

Exchanging questions that have no answer for questions that do is an act of surrender. There comes a point of surrendering our demand to know why. Some might say settling for not getting our questions answered is a negative response. But is it? Does surrendering our questions mean we're settling for something less? One definition of "to settle" means "to be quiet and calm." Peace enters when we let go of our demand for answers. I'd say that's settling for more, not less.

MILEPOST 87
HOW CAN I POSSIBLY BELIEVE GOD IS GOOD?

If God is good, why does He allow tragedy? From the ordinary person on the street to the theologian in seminary school, we all want to know the answer to the question of why bad things happen. Books delve deeply into the subject, but only a few seem to satisfy our need to understand.

I remember the first time I really grappled with this question. A friend of mine had just taken her own life. The day before, we had lunch together, and I still remember our conversation. If only I had known what she was contemplating, I'd take back everything I said and say something completely different. Perhaps it wouldn't have helped. I will never know. But I cried out to God, "I didn't know what she was planning to do, but God, You did. Why didn't You stop her?"

His answer? "How do you know I didn't try?" That can sometimes be a tough answer to swallow.

What do we do with all the Scriptures about God's protection when it looks as if He failed? What do we do with all the Scriptures about healing when healing didn't come? What do we do when there seems to be no rhyme or reason for what happened?

We could go the way of atheists and say there is no God. We could follow agnostics and say that maybe there is a God, but He (or she, as some might say) is impersonal, doesn't get involved with us, and doesn't care. We could blame sin or blame it on not saying the right prayer or not doing the right ritual or not having enough faith. But in the end, blame changes nothing. We are still no closer to really understanding why. Like it or not, that is often the reality of it. We simply don't have answers. That reality raises another question. *Can we accept the mystery? Can we trust God even when we don't understand?* Is God good only when the sun shines? Is proof of God's goodness only if nothing bad happens? Or is proof of His goodness evident in how greatly He comforts and strengthens us and walks with us in our darkest hour? Maybe a greater miracle is in seeing how God transforms the tragedy into a triumph.

Everything I believe and know of God keeps me from blaming Him for what happened. God didn't do this to us or to our daughter. God didn't "take" her. Nor did God "need another angel in Heaven" or "another flower in His garden." As common as those sayings are at funerals and from well-intentioned friends, that sort of thinking points accusingly at God, calling Him a thief, which is not at all helpful, correct, or true.

We often say things like, "God is good," and "God is love," but when tragedy enters our lives, we have an opportunity to discover if we really believe it. Love and goodness are more than mere *qualities* of God. They are His very *being*. It is impossible for God to be otherwise. Our confidence is built on the bedrock of His love and goodness as steadfast and sure—even when bad things happen.

I might not be able to explain why things happen as they do, but I can rely on the certainty of God's love, compassion, and help in times of trouble. He is indeed our refuge, our strength, our fortress, and our salvation. I can believe God is good, because He's *proven* himself faithful through every day of my life, including the day Jeanette went to Heaven.

"Truly he is my rock and my salvation; he is my fortress, I will not be shaken. My salvation and my honor depend on God; he is my mighty rock, my refuge. Trust in him at all times, you people; pour out your hearts to him, for God is our refuge" (Psalm 62:6–8).

MILEPOST 88
EARTH'S GRIEF AND HEAVEN'S GLORY

Through Jesus, therefore, let us continually offer to God a sacrifice of praise—the fruit of lips that openly profess his name (Hebrews 13:15).

Since Jeanette's been gone, Heaven is in my thoughts more than ever before. I reflect on the many contrasts between life as it is here and life as it is in Heaven. I meditate on promises that God will wipe away all tears from our eyes, and there won't be any more death or sorrow or grief (Revelation 21: 4). All the painful aspects of this life will end, and we'll never go through troubles again. Sometimes, I sit and think about what life must be like for Jeanette in that kind of atmosphere.

Thoughts about my own Heaven-going are set against a backdrop of Bible verses that speak of offering God a sacrifice of praise. I don't feel much like singing a praise song when my heart is breaking. Yes, it certainly can be a sacrifice—a definite mental and spiritual discipline—to praise and thank God while I'm walking through this grief journey.

However, a new thought is stirring in me about the contrast between life here on earth and life in Heaven. All our earthly troubles will be over in Heaven. We'll be in His presence where worship, thanks, and praise will spring forth from us freely and easily because everything that hinders worship here on earth will be gone. Praise and thanksgiving will be as natural as breathing in Heaven.

Doesn't that bring more depth of meaning to our sacrifices of praise and thanks here in this life? Isn't it more significant to worship God even when we don't feel like it—even through tears, even with our broken hearts—than praising God in Heaven where it's no sacrifice at all? Here and now in this earthly realm is the only chance we get to push past our sorrows, griefs, troubles, questions, worries, fears, and negativity to worship God, because in Heaven those hinderances won't exist. When we get to Heaven, we will no longer have the opportunity we do now for that kind of devotion in worship and thanksgiving.

Our sacrifices of praise and thanksgiving are part of the treasure we're storing in Heaven. Here in this life is the only place we get to produce and store up that kind of treasure. How should that thought affect our outlook, our attitudes, and our grief journey?

MILEPOST 89
GRIEF SUPPORT GROUPS

Friendship is born at that moment when one person says to another: What! You too? I thought I was the only one. – C. S. Lewis[18]

This classic C. S. Lewis quote captures so well what a good support group is all about—knowing we are not alone, knowing others are experiencing the same types of struggles we are, and being able to talk about it with those who get it. And, yes, many friendships grow from our group.

People often ask what we do at a grief support group meeting. Some have wondered why we would want to sit around and talk about our loss. Doesn't talking about it remind us of our loss even more? How we can stand to discuss such serious, heavy topics? How is that helpful? You might be surprised.

Here's a picture of what a strong support group should look like. A grief support group is not counseling. It's a place for sharing, so most of all, it should be safe.

People should be able to speak openly and honestly and be accepted wherever they are in their journey. People should be loved and accepted unconditionally. God loves and accepts us where we are, but He also doesn't want us to remain stuck there. Likewise, as we build a bridge of trust and acceptance, we can help others walk out of unhealthy places of hurt and pain.

All sharing in a support group should remain confidential. What is shared with the group stays in the group. Sometimes I do share anecdotes about our group so others will understand what we do but without mentioning names or identifying details. Some people in the group have no qualms of sharing their stories, but everyone doesn't feel the same way, and they need assurance that nothing will leave the room without their permission.

Sharing time is a major part of meetings, but it's best to have books, podcasts, or videos to discuss as well. We know we're not alone in our struggles when we read or hear other people's stories, and they teach us helpful strategies and ways to cope and overcome.

Some kind of closing ritual is a soothing benediction after all we've talked about in a meeting. This closes the gathering with a sense of releasing the burdens we've been carrying so we can depart with peace. Some groups light a candle and pass it around while sharing a brief thought about our loved one. I like closing my group with communion, remembering that Jesus was a "Man of Sorrows, acquainted with grief," and that He carried our griefs and sorrows so we can be healed (Isaiah 53:3–5).

I encourage people to find a grief support group if there's one available. Often, groups meet in churches or as part of community mental health resources. We'll come to a point in our grief journey when we're ready to meet with a group. My husband and I were invited to a group almost immediately after our daughter's death. We only attended a few times and stopped going. A couple of years passed before I began attending another group. At the time of attending the first group, we were still in too much shock and denial, still trying to wrap our heads around the fact that our daughter was gone. It was too soon. However, when I started attending the second group, I found it refreshing and restoring, and I loved it. It depends on finding the right group at the right time. You can also find online grief support groups, and they can be helpful, too. But the interpersonal interaction of a group you meet with in person can further promote healing if one is open and ready.

MILEPOST 90
LIFE'S DEFINING MOMENTS

I'm sure you've heard the expression, "When life hands you lemons, make lemonade." Squeezing lemons gives you lemon juice, but it takes a whole lot of sugar to turn that sour juice into lemonade. It's not so different with us. When we're squeezed by tragedy, it may take a whole lot of sweetener to make the sour taste palatable.

One lemon-juice-to-lemonade story is of Job and of how he responded to the tragedies that descended on him. In a single day, he lost everything. His immediate response was, "Naked I came from my mother's womb, and naked I will depart. The Lord gave and the Lord has taken away; may the name of the Lord be praised" (Job 1:21). He recognized that we have nothing when we enter this world, and when we exit, no worldly goods acquired in life go with us. Job's story is all about people grappling with the whys of tragedy, and it's a great case study. The stage is set in the introduction of the book by a scene in heaven that makes clear all the troubles that afflict Job come from one source: Satan. But Job and his friends aren't privy to that scene, so instead, they come up with all sorts of explanations, blaming everyone, including Job himself. Isn't that just like us? We want an explanation so badly, we often reach the wrong conclusions.

When God finally spoke directly to Job, He did not answer the question of "why." Yet Job was thoroughly satisfied with God's response. Job replied, "Surely I spoke of things I did not understand, things too wonderful for me to know. My ears had heard of you but now my eyes have seen you" (Job 42:3–4). Between the beginning and the end of Job's story, Job came to know God in a new way. And then, God poured more abundant blessings into Job's life than he had before. That's what God does. Although He didn't prevent Satan's destruction, He blessed Job in even greater measure. Through this drama, God demonstrated that Satan doesn't win in the end. The tables will be turned on him, and *God* gets the victory!

If Job had given into his wife's advice to "curse God and die" or if he had succumbed to the despair and guilt heaped on him by his friends, his name would not be recorded in history, and we would never have heard of him. Instead, he hung on to his faith in God against all the winds of adversity and loss. This was his defining moment, and it's such a profound story of faith, we still read about him and know of him today.

Now fast forward a few thousand years from Job to Jesus. In the beginning of Job's story, we're told of the interaction between God and Satan, but there's more. As Jesus hung on the cross and Satan celebrated his supposed win, Jesus spoke three final words, "It is finished!" (John 19:30). Jesus might as well have said, "Satan, you lose! You do not get the last word!" Through His death, burial, and resurrection, Jesus shattered Satan's power. This was Jesus's defining moment.

Does evil still exist in the world? Yes, and tragedies do happen, but Satan still doesn't get the last word. These life events become our defining moments. What will we do when tragedy strikes? The death of our child is probably the hardest thing we'll ever face. But Jesus's victory on the cross stands between us and our tragedy. Job didn't have that, but we do. We have the resurrection power of Jesus so that we can stand and be victorious.

When life squeezes us painfully, even brutally, we have a choice to remain sour or let the sweetening grace of Jesus turn it into lemonade. Our greatest loss can become our greatest victory. This is our defining moment.

"Let this hope burst forth within you, releasing a continual joy. Don't give up in a time of trouble, but commune with God at all times .... Never let evil defeat you, but defeat evil with good" (Romans 12:12, 21 TPT). "Even in times of trouble we have a joyful confidence, knowing that our pressures will develop in us patient endurance. And patient endurance will refine our character, and proven character leads us back to hope. And this hope is not a disappointing fantasy, because we can now experience the endless love of God cascading into our hearts through the Holy Spirit who lives in us" (Romans 5:3–5 TPT).

Footsteps to Survive and Thrive

One thread running through this entire book has been the choices we make. We can be bitter about what happened, or we can use it as a steppingstone to rise higher and to be better, more compassionate, and more intentional in our living. We can let ourselves be drawn into darkness, or we can seek light, follow light, and be a light for others. We can think positively or negatively. We are the master of our conscious thoughts and choices. We can't control some things: We can't turn back the clock or undo what happened. We can't control the season of grief we've entered, but we can control our response to it and how we choose to travel through it.

After all is said and done, there is only one thing anyone really needs to know about how to survive and thrive through their grief journey: to know God, to spend time with Him in intimate fellowship, and to stay so closely connected with Him that we know He's holding us in His arms at all times and through every storm. When everything else fades and all that remains is love and trust, we will have found the true secret of survival. God is our source and the wellspring of all hope.

The one thing most necessary to carry us through the storms of our grief is intimacy with God. We need time for quietness to listen and hear the Holy Spirit speak in our hearts. The world is a noisy place, plus the noise of our own thoughts is constantly in our heads. We need to learn how to practice stillness in the presence of God so the cacophony of all that noise is silenced. In a quiet place that's just between ourselves and God, we find grace, we find strength, we find comfort, we find peace, and we find everything we need to survive and thrive. Stillness is a rare commodity these days. It's a treasure to seek, but it can be found. If we're seeking God, we will find Him (Matthew 7:7–11). That's a promise. No matter how thick the darkness seems, God's light can always be found by those who seek.

"God is our refuge and strength, an ever-present help in trouble. Therefore we will not fear, though the earth give way and the mountains fall into the heart of the sea, though its waters roar and foam and the mountains quake with their surging. There is a river whose streams make glad the city of God, the holy place where the Most High dwells. God is within her, she will not fall; God will help her at break of day" (Psalm 46:1–5).

ACKNOWLEDGMENTS

I would not have accomplished any number of things in life without my husband's confidence in my ability to succeed. In writing this book, the biggest endeavor of my life, he believed in me every step of the way. We've walked this grief journey together, and this is his story as much as mine. Thank you, Dennis, for never giving up and helping me to never give up.

I'm so grateful for my best friend, Linda, who has walked every mile of this journey with me, for her comfort, unconditional love, encouragement, prayers, and faithful friendship.

Equally heartfelt thanks to Sylvia and my Good News Girls sisters, my Artlings Book and Crafts Group, and my Footsteps of Hope Grief Support Group. Thank you for your encouragement, grace, love, and support throughout this journey.

Thanks also to my editor, Lisa Thompson, and others who supplied input throughout the editorial and revision process. You helped make it a much better book than I could have achieved alone.

ABOUT THE AUTHOR

Sara Nelson grew up in rural Iowa and Wisconsin. After she married her husband, Dennis, they lived and traveled in Europe, Panama, and many states across the country as a military family. Sara taught elementary and middle school grades in Christian school for fifteen years.

In 2018, she co-authored a book called *Pirate's Tower* with David Washburn. *Pirate's Tower* is a mysterious and intriguing time-travel adventure. Themes of hope, faith, and trust in the goodness of God permeate Sara's writing. She authentically testifies to the goodness of God, not because He keeps bad things from happening, but because He strengthens us, comforts us, weeps with us, walks with us, and carries us through, enabling us to overcome whatever happens.

Sara enjoys nature, camping, and travel—especially road trips in search of off-the-beaten-path sights, Americana, nostalgia, and adventures. At home, Sara loves getting together with friends over coffee, conversation, and laughter.

Coming Books by Sara Faith Nelson

Footsteps of Discovery: Exploring the Kingdom of God

RECOMMENDED RESOURCES

From Laura Diehl and GPS Hope (**G**rieving **P**arents **S**haring Hope)—www.gpshope.org

When Tragedy Strikes: Rebuilding Your Life with Hope and Healing after the Death of Your Child

Reflections of Hope: Daily Readings for Bereaved Parents

Hope for the Future: An Advent Journey for Bereaved Parents

Come Grieve Through Our Eyes: How to Give Comfort and Support to Bereaved Parents by Taking a Glimpse into Our Hidden World of Grief

REFERENCES

1. Pamela D. Blair and Brook Noel, *I Wasn't Ready to Say Good Bye: Surviving, Coping, and Healing After the Sudden Death of a Loved One* (Naperville, Illinois: Sourcebooks, Inc., 2008).

2. Laura Diehl, "I Am Afraid I Am Losing my Mind," August 13, 2019, in *Facing Our Fears After the Death of Our Child*, podcast, "Grieving Parents Sharing Hope," www.gpshope.org/podcast/17/.

3. Patricia Connelly, et al., *Worlds to Explore: Handbook for Brownie and Junior Girl Scouts* (New York City: Girl Scouts of the USA, 1977).

4. Nicholson, William, screenwriter and Attenborough, Richard, dir. *Shadowlands* (Savoy Pictures & Paramount Pictures, 1993).

5. B. Davenport and S. J. Scott, *Effortless Journaling: How to Start a Journal, Make It a Habit, and Find Endless Writing Topics* (Virginia: Oldtown Publishing LLC, 2018).

6. Paul Necri, ed., *101 Great American Poems* (New York: Dover Publications, Inc., 1998).

7. Todd Burpo, *Heaven is for Real: A Little Boy's Astounding Story of his Trip to Heaven and Back* (Nashville: Thomas Nelson. 2011).

8. C. S. Lewis, *The Last Battle* (New York: MacMillan Publishing, 1956), 160.

9. John Bunyon, *The Pilgrim's Progress* (Unknown: Coterie Classics, 2016).

10. Reinhold Niebuhr, "Prayer for Serenity," *Celebrate Recovery*, Accessed March 11, 2019, www.celebraterecovery.com/resources/cr-tools/serenityprayer.

11. Ibid.

12. C. S. Lewis, *A Grief Observed* (New York: Harper Collins, 1961,1996), 3.

13. Linda Ellis, *Live Your Dash: Make Every Moment Matter* (New York: Sterling Ethos, 2011).

14. J. R. R. Tolkien and Douglas Anderson, *The Annotated Hobbit* (California: Houghton Mifflin. 2002), 32.

15. Spanberger, Keith. (Church sermon, Shiloh Christian Ministries, Sierra Vista, AZ, September 22, 2019).

16. "Miscarriage," Mayo Clinic, accessed November 16, 2019, https://www.mayoclinic.org/diseases-conditions/pregnancy-loss-miscarriage/symptoms-causes/syc-20354298.

17. Ackerman, Andy, dir. *Seinfeld*. Episode 166, "The Strike." Aired December 18, 1997, on NBC.

18. C. S. Lewis, *The Four Loves* (Harper Collins: NY, 1960), 83.

www.ingramcontent.com/pod-product-compliance
Lightning Source LLC
LaVergne TN
LVHW021652060526
838200LV00050B/2314